I Don't
Want to Have
the
Prayer

*A Messy
Pastor's Kid
Does Her
Memory Work*

I Don't
Want to Have
the
Prayer

KAREN KUHLMANN AVERITT

YELLOW TABLET
PRESS

For information about this title or to order other books
and/or electronic media, contact the publisher:

Yellow Tablet Press
833 SW Lemans Lane, Suite 189
Lee's Summit, MO 64082
www.yellowtabletpress.com

Library of Congress Control Number: 2020902594

ISBNs:
978-1-7343380-0-3 (Paperback)
978-1-7343380-2-7 (Hardcover)
978-1-7343380-1-0 (eBook)

Printed in the United States of America

Cover and Interior design: 1106 Design

For my husband and our son

In memory of my dad, Marv, who was exactly as he seemed,
and my mom, Donna, who was far more than she appeared.
She is the star of this show.

Table of Contents

Introduction

Frequently Asked Questions

I've fielded many weird and intrusive questions throughout my life as a Lutheran pastor's kid. Something about that part of my identity often obliterated the polite boundaries of social discourse. When I was younger, questions from my peers were irritating enough, but adults asked ridiculous ones, too. They still do. They want to know about my teenage rebellion or the strange religious rites my family engaged in behind closed doors. Here are some of their questions and, because my parents are no longer around to advise me to keep a lid on the sass, my answers to them:

- ❧ "So, are you an angel or a bad girl?" Do I have to be one or the other?

- ❧ "You know what I've heard about girls like you?" Messy, bookish, introverted girls like me? *Wait, what have you heard?*

❧ "Does your dad wear his robe all the time?" Yes, you should see him in it when he changes the oil in his car or mows the lawn.

❧ "Do you pray all the time at home?" 24/7 if I've spilled cranberry juice on my mom's new couch.

❧ "Are you adopted?" My brother told me I was and said papers were in the attic to prove it.

❧ "Were your parents celibate?" I wish. That would have kept me from overhearing them not being celibate one time when I showed up, unannounced, at their house.

❧ "Does your dad need to eat and sleep like regular people?" Yes, because he is, in fact, a human being and not a mythical creature.

❧ "Where does a pastor go on vacation?" As far away as he can get.

❧ "How does your dad justify working only two hours a week?" They are an intense two hours.

❧ "Do you automatically go to Heaven?" Yes, but not because my dad was a pastor. Jesus paid my way. Give Him a chance— He'll change your life.

Chapter One

Home Place

Dad, left, with his brothers
Harland and Dale, c. 1938

My dad, Marv (Marvin, actually, but he detested that name),
grew up during the Great Depression in Chester, Nebraska,
a farming community in the central part of the state, eight miles
north of the Kansas border. Dad's fondness for his hometown was
so palpable that my brother Brent and I grew up believing it was the
greatest place on earth. Named for President Chester A. Arthur, the

town's primary claim to fame is six-man football, which a Chester High School coach conceived in 1934. This variation of the sport allowed high schools lacking enough students for the requisite eleven players on offense and defense to field football teams.[1]

Chester is typical of many small towns in the Midwest, founded during the railroad boom and now hanging on despite a poor economy and the need to drive sixty miles to York, Nebraska, for a Starbucks latte. In some ways, Chester hasn't changed much since the 1930s. The farm that belonged to three generations of my family before being sold is still there. Two churches—Lutheran and Methodist—remain. Most residents are white and of German descent, and cornfields planted in fertile black soil encircle the town. This was the Promised Land for immigrants like my great-grandparents who arrived in the late 1800s. Now it's the proverbial wide spot in the road—a road that bypasses the business district and takes people to places that time and technology haven't left behind.

I was back there a few years ago for my Uncle Paul's funeral on a dismal December day; a cold rain made the town seem more derelict than usual. Several businesses I remembered from my childhood visits were gone: The Sundowner Bar and Grill, Rosie's Café, and Navis's General Store. I loved tagging along to Navis's with my grandmother, who wore her Sunday dress to purchase the Carnation powdered milk, spumoni ice cream, and instant tea that were staples on the farm. The tiny store, with its dark wood floors and the friendly butcher behind the meat counter, was exotic compared to our A&P at home.

St. John Lutheran Church, where my extended family worshipped, no longer operates an elementary school. *The Chester*

Herald newspaper is defunct, and the Chester public school building was purchased on eBay by a Las Vegas artist and her husband, who turned it into The Center of Creativity—a place for the locals to get their art on. This development surprised me when I first heard about it. The Chester I know doesn't strike me as a hotbed of the creative arts, and the residents look askance at people from Omaha, not to mention Sin City. Relatives tell me that the center offers workshops in lamp and clock making. The next Jasper Johns or Roy Lichtenstein probably won't come from one of these classes, but I'm confident The Center of Creativity has injected life into the town.

A person can still buy a comfortable house in Chester for less than what he or she would pay for a new, fully-loaded Ford F-150 truck. When I tell my son that I want to acquire a vacation home in Chester, he begs me to admit I'm joking, and I am. Sort of. While Chester is in many ways the modern suburbanite's nightmare with its lack of, oh, just about everything, it still possesses a mythic quality for my brother and me. Our dad's stories of growing up during the Depression and World War II painted a picture of an American idyll marred only by stern old-world relatives. As pastor's kids, we moved several times during our childhoods, so we never had a hometown, a single spot we could point to on a map and say, "That's where I grew up." We were raised in parsonages, houses that weren't our homes. They belonged to the congregations our dad served, which was made abundantly clear when the garbage disposal stopped working, and we had to wait for the church property board to authorize the repair. I suppose, for my brother and me, the farm at Chester is our home place, our touchstone of family and faith.

Chester made my dad who he was as a man and as a pastor. I can separate him from a lot of people and a lot of places, but never from Chester. Dad was genuinely upbeat and ready to see the adventure in any circumstance. He even reminisced with fondness about the Depression and Dust Bowl years. Admittedly, his family, though they worked hard for what they had, wasn't destitute like so many others in the 1930s.

My great-grandfather, John Christian Kuhlmann, brought his wife Minnie and their nine surviving children to Chester from Champaign, Illinois, shortly after my grandfather Walter, the youngest of the family, was born in 1897. John Christian, a German immigrant, ran a successful general store in Champaign but wanted to give farming a go. He either was a farming savant or had saved lots of cash from his retail enterprise back in Illinois because he gave each of his children, girls included, a debt-free quarter section (160 acres) farm when they reached adulthood. My grandpa eventually took over his parents' farm. Both my Kuhlmann great-grandparents died long before I was born, and few photos of them exist. The two pictures I have of Minnie are creepy. One shows her draped in black and standing in a thicket of trees, her bony fingers clasping her shawl as she scowls at the camera. In the other, she is, again, cloaked in black, peering at something from behind the corner of the house—like maybe a couple of kids whom she can lure back to her house for fattening up before roasting them for dinner.

"She liked to lurk in the shadows," my dad told me. "We felt like we were being watched whenever she was around."

The greatest influence on my dad while growing up was his mother's side of the family—the Grabaus. They had come to America in the 1890s from tiny Kuhstedtermoor, Germany, where they had been peat farmers. The Grabaus had forty boggy acres from which they harvested peat and dried it into bricks before hauling it by boat to the port of Bremerhaven for shipment to London where it was sold as fuel for stoves. That's what our cousin Ingrid explained to my parents and me on a visit to Dad's ancestral home where she and her husband, Jürgen, gave us a tour of their local peat museum that displays the tools my relatives used to harvest peat before they abandoned them for the good life in Nebraska. You might think peat exhibits would be excruciatingly dull. They're not. They are only mind-numbingly dull.

Ingrid's great-grandfather, Heinrich, and my dad's grandfather were siblings. There were thirteen children in the family: Katharina the First, Diedrich the First, Klaus, Meta, Anna, Heinrich, Adelheide, Johann, Herman, Gesina, Adeline, Katharina the Second, and Diedrich the Second. The two oldest died young, as noted in the family Bible, from a "disease that swept Germany." I don't know if the two youngest kids were named to honor their departed siblings or if their parents had run out of names by that point. Heinrich was the only sibling who remained in Germany—peat farming must have been his passion. Everyone else and their spouses and children immigrated en masse to the United States. Klaus and Meta settled their families in Brooklyn, and the other nine families headed west.

Following our tour of the peat museum, Ingrid and her husband took us to the nearby municipal park. At its center was a monument to the town's fallen World War II soldiers. There were scores of names on the memorial—many of whom died as young as thirteen, Hitler having become desperate enough to conscript children as the war dragged on. Ingrid picked this odd moment and place to ask my dad if he wished he had grown up in Germany. My dad turned to consider the war memorial, then looked back at Ingrid.

"Nein," he succinctly, but kindly, answered his clearly disappointed cousin.

"Honestly, Ingrid! Marvin would be *dead* now if he had grown up here!" my mom, who understood German but couldn't speak a word of it, declared.

Ingrid, the rare modern German who doesn't speak multiple languages, didn't comprehend my mom's emphatic reaction, and she announced it was time to head back to her house where we drank coffee, avoided unpleasant topics of conversation, and tried to make a dent in the six cakes she had baked for us.

My great-grandparents, Johann and Gesche (rhymes with fishy), had four living children: Heinrich, Johann, Ernest, and Hulda. The boys answered to their German names only at home and around older relatives. Otherwise, they were Hank, John, and Ernie. My grandma couldn't do anything with the name Hulda, so she was stuck with it. She and Uncle Ernie were born in Nebraska, as were the three children of whom no one spoke: Ella Mathilda, Arthur, and Infant.

6

My parents, brother, and I often visited Chester over Memorial Day weekend. I loved going with Grandma to the cemetery, where we placed Mason jars packed with magenta peonies on the family graves. When I was old enough to note the small headstones with three unfamiliar names, I quizzed her.

"Who are Ella Mathilda and Arthur, and why didn't anybody name the baby?" I asked.

"They were some children who died," Grandma answered.

"Whose children?"

"Hmm?"

"Grandma, whose children were they, and why did they die?" I demanded.

"They were young children."

I was getting nowhere with her. I had to wait for answers until we returned to the farm. By the age of three, I had figured out the Old-World German Relatives Code of Conduct, which included the rule that sad things must never be mentioned. Merely unpleasant things may be addressed in German while sports, weather, swap radio, and crops may be discussed at length and in English.

"Who were Ella Mathilda, Arthur, and the baby nobody bothered to give a name?" I asked my dad when I had the chance to corner him in private.

"Who?"

"The little tombstones in the cemetery. Grandma won't tell me."

Now my dad understood. "I'm fairly sure they're her younger brother and sister, but I don't know if the baby was a boy or girl," Dad answered.

"Why don't you know?"

"She never answered me when I asked, and I'm certain that when those children died, they were never mentioned again."

I never met my great-grandmother Gesche, but her photo makes me think I would have adored her like I did my grandma. Plump and smiling, mischief in her eyes, she looked completely opposite of my other great-grandmother, the Ringwraith. Gesche and my dad were particularly close, and he spent afternoons at her farm, helping around the house and snacking on lard sandwiches and pickled pig's feet. Gesche didn't speak English, and it was at her table that Dad honed his German language skills. She loved to joke and laugh, which set her apart from the scores of dour relatives in Chester, and she doted on the grandson who, she told her family, "was the most American-acting but most German-looking" of the lot. My dad, with his blond hair and ice-blue eyes, looked like the prototype model of a Hitler Youth recruiting poster.

If I had lost three young children as Gesche had lost hers, I would be bitter. I might even go to church only for the opportunity to be ticked at God on His own turf, but my great-grandmother remained faithful. She continued to worship when her movie-star handsome son, John, died in a car accident two weeks before his planned wedding to his childhood sweetheart. And Gesche was back in church the Sunday after her husband was killed when horses that were harnessed to the thresher he was using became spooked, and they bolted, pulling him into the machine. It would have been easy for Gesche to accuse God of cruelty, but she never bought into the whole "Where was God when?" thing. Her trust in her Savior was absolute, and the young boy eating lard sandwiches at her table couldn't fail to notice.

Gesche was not only a counterpoint to Dad's paternal grand-mother, but she also stood in contrast to her brother's wife, Aunt Lena. Lena was a stout, grumpy woman, and her whippet-thin, henpecked husband, Gevert, moved through life sad and defeated. According to my dad, their relationship consisted of Lena screaming orders and complaints, while Gevert took her abuse and complied with her dictates. Lena should have stayed behind in Germany to help with peat farming because she didn't like her new country. She was another one who refused to learn English, believing God would no longer be able to understand her prayers. Granted, the language can be perplexing. I like to picture God on His sapphire throne, puzzling over its idiosyncrasies.

"Creating the universe from nothing and redeeming mankind was a piece of cake, but I wish people wouldn't pray in English. It's confusing."

See how God used an English idiom? He has this covered.

Despite her lack of confidence in God's language skills, Lena was a strident, pious Lutheran. So committed to her denomination was she, that next to her bed she kept a framed photo of the Lutheran Hour radio show speaker, Dr. Walter A. Maier. She cradled his photo during the weekly broadcast from St. Louis, which, even though the program was in English, she listened to without fail. Dr. Maier was a dazzling preaching talent with a vast theological resume, and sixty-something Lena had a crush on him. She said "Guten Morgen" to his photo when she awakened, and she wished him "Gute Nacht" when she went to bed. He wasn't, however, her only pretend boyfriend. She kept another man's photo in a frame on her nightstand, and, unlike Dr. Maier, this charismatic speaker did his radio broadcasts in German. From Berlin.

"So, your aunt secretly rooted for Germany during the war?" I asked my dad.

"No," he replied. "It wasn't a secret."

Lena acted as midwife when my dad, two years younger than his brother Harland, was born at home in 1931. My grandpa and sad Uncle Gevert busied themselves outside so that they didn't have to think about the obstetrical matters going on in the first-floor bedroom. Two years later, my Uncle Dale was born, and the triad of mischief was complete. Their two youngest siblings, Paul and Dorothy, came along years later. When Dorothy was born, Aunt Lena told the older boys, almost teenagers, that the angels had brought them a baby sister. The boys had been tending livestock for years and were hip to how babies were made. Lena explained the origins of babies differently with each birth. Special newborns, like Aunt Dorothy, arrived via heavenly host while others were delivered via stork. Less worthy children, according to Lena, were found in the cabbage patch.

The farm provided equal amounts of work and fun for the three oldest, rambunctious boys. They were responsible for cleaning the barns, helping plant and harvest crops, and feeding and butchering livestock. My dad was proud that he had been a whiz at hog butchering, a skill he counted as one of the best he'd ever learned. I once made the mistake of asking him about the process over dinner. I was okay until he described the lungs and what was done with them. I concentrated on keeping my dinner down as my parents sat there savoring their food and trading tales of slaughter and offal.

As a 4-H member, Dad raised a calf every year to show at the county fair. The box of blue ribbons I found after his death testifies that he did a good job. A few ribbons were from the American Royal—the big deal annual livestock show and auction held at the Kansas City stockyards. At least once, Dad's calf won the grand prize. Or was it a steer by then? I don't know the appropriate terms for farm animals. I go to the store and buy a package of 96 percent lean ground beef, blissfully unaware of the stages of the source's life cycle. Anyway, my dad was awarded a sizeable check for his win, and the raised-from-infancy animal was turned over to a slaughterhouse. My grandpa treated my dad to dinner before they headed to whichever flophouse they were lodging in that year.

Unlike many Americans, my dad's family didn't experience true poverty during the Depression. Although they didn't have cash to spend on extras, my grandpa, having received his parents' farm free and clear, worked hard to stay in the black. Meat was plentiful, a large garden provided a surplus of vegetables, and dozens of fruit trees and wild berry bushes yielded enough peaches, cherries, apples, and gooseberries to stock the cellar. Grandma patched threadbare clothing, and extra income went into the offering plate at church or into the bank if any cash remained after tithing. Even in 1936, one of the hottest and driest years on record, the Kuhlmanns were okay. They had enough to eat, and no one could take away their land.

For cheap entertainment, Dad and his brothers walked to town most afternoons and spent a half-hour gazing at the bottles of iced-down orange pop that filled the metal tub in front of the general store. By the time my dad was ten years old, the boys were smoking cigarettes, stealing their much older cousin Eddie's car, and joyriding to town. (I freaked out with worry when my strapping son wanted to ride his bike to a convenience store two miles from our home—when he was fifteen.)

My dad's lungs weren't so healthy in his later years, but he was from a generation that knew how to adult. He and his brothers, along with Dad's best friend Donnie Elwell, weren't helicoptered—maybe because their respective parents were too busy to worry about things like the ubiquitous farm combination of bare feet, rusty nails, and the lack of tetanus vaccinations. My dad once sliced halfway down the length of his foot with a corn knife when he was chasing a mouse through a field. The wound prompted a rare trip to the doctor, but it didn't slow him down or cause his parents to implement new rules about the responsible handling of a tool *that looks like a machete.* Furthermore, the boys were children—the oldest was in third grade, tops—when they went out alone to hunt and fish. Dad had a shotgun before he had most of his permanent teeth.

Chapter Two

Superstition, War, and a Cruel German Shepherd

Dad's confirmation photo, 1945

Although my Grandma Kuhlmann usually epitomized gentleness and calm, she could be strangely fearful and superstitious. To be fair, the deaths of four siblings and her father must have caused her anxiety, and she legitimately was concerned that her sons were going to kill themselves or each other while doing something stupid. I get that—I'm a mother. But some of her fears were cultural, and many of my German relatives had strange notions. Aunt Maggie, for example, wouldn't allow anyone to open an umbrella indoors for fear it would precipitate a death in the family. Another aunt was convinced that when large numbers of crows assembled, they could be heard cawing the words "komm mit"—German for "come with." She said it meant someone was going to die. Once, when we were all gathered outside at the farm to cook some burgers, smoke from the grill swirled upward in what Grandma thought was an ominous manner.

"Something bad is going to happen," she warned.

"Is somebody going to die?" I asked cheekily. What *didn't* signal impending death or catastrophe to my relatives?

"Maybe not right away," she answered.

But more than strange signs, what really disturbed my relatives were cats. Most elderly German people I know detest cats. Maybe they were taught, like my brother and I were, that felines possess supernatural powers of persuasion along with a potent bloodlust— particularly for babies.

Three "truths" Brent and I learned from both sets of grandparents:

1. A cat will jump into a crib and steal a baby's breath. This was described by Grandma Kuhlmann in detail as a sort of reverse mouth-to-mouth resuscitation.

2. If you walk up any stairs on which a cat is sitting and, doubtless, plotting, the cat will deliberately trip you so that

you fall down the stairs—resulting in great injury to you and smug satisfaction for the cat.

3. Never look directly at a cat. It will maintain eye contact and hypnotize you. It was never explained to me what devious things the cat would persuade me to do once I was bent to its will, but I steered clear of the kittens in the barnyard.

Despite their sincere Christian faith, my Kuhlmann grand-parents' fear of car accidents, illness, and death rendered them so timid that they rarely ventured more than two miles from home. My dad once said that they were "two people who wouldn't leave the farm if there was a lone, small cloud anywhere over Thayer County, Nebraska." Again, because of her father's grisly end and her brother's early death, I understand why my grandmother was such a worrier; but it annoyed me when she used fear tactics rather than logic in urging others to caution.

For example, instead of telling me to be careful when I wanted to walk out to the farm's largest pond in a far pasture, Grandma told me the story of a boy from town who went missing after wandering from home. His parents, not knowing where he had gone, looked several days for him until someone suggested dredging the very pond on my grandparents' farm to which I now wanted to stroll. Searchers worked for hours until his lifeless eight-year-old body was brought out and given to his heartbroken parents.

"His name was Richard," Grandma said. "Have a nice walk down to the pond."

Although my grandparents' German-ness manifested itself in their weird belief in omens, it didn't turn them into the prickly variety of German like Aunt Lena or Hans Kortes, a traveling salesman who showed up at the farm every few weeks. Hans, who came to the U.S. following World War I, had an outgoing personality along with a large suitcase containing scarves, neckties, and kitchen gadgets. My grandma never bought much, but she always invited Hans into the house for coffee and cake, providing him the opportunity to speak longingly about the Fatherland and how hard it was to find a good German girl to marry. Hans was intimidated by the girls in Chester. They were silly first-generation or, even worse, second-generation Americans who spoke perfect English and were put off by his unsuccessful attempts at fluency and courtship. He wanted a solid and serious immigrant bride with a thick accent to match his own.

My dad, around five years old at the time, idolized Hans Kortes and wanted to emulate the salesman, so he appropriated a dilapidated suitcase from the attic and pretended to sell gadgets and clothing accessories to all the relatives. My grandma, thinking this was precious, told Hans about it during one of his sales calls. She asked my dad to come into the kitchen to demonstrate how he "played Hans Kortes." Dad did a credible job with the sales pitch, which he conducted in German. But instead of being flattered or amused, Hans was outraged. He grabbed the suitcase, stormed outside, and kicked it to pieces.

"Es gibt nur eine Hans Kortes!" (There is only one Hans Kortes!) he screamed, shaking his fist at my startled dad before grabbing his own suitcase and leaving without thanking Grandma for dessert.

Hans returned only once, and he didn't bring his kit of goods. Instead, he announced that he was moving to western Nebraska to open a general store. He thought that would suit him better than door-to-door sales, and he hoped there would be fewer assimilated girls in that part of the state. Years later, Grandma heard that Hans ran a successful business and had found a nice girl to marry. Since there were no reports of him smashing some kid's play cash register, Hans must have found some measure of happiness.

During World War II, several thousand German prisoners of war, most of whom were captured in North Africa, were held at Camp Concordia, a prison camp located about twenty-five miles south of Chester. The POWs worked on area farms to compensate for the numbers of farm workers who were serving with the Allied forces. On weekdays, camp personnel trucked a group of prisoners to the Kuhlmann farm, where they worked alongside the family in the fields and were invited to eat lunch with them in the kitchen. The POWs must have felt at home among people who spoke their language. My grandma felt sorry for these men and for their starving families back home, so she often packed parcels of coffee and tea and mailed them to Germany along with the care packages she sent to her hungry relatives back on the peat farm. Sometimes she even made flour sack dresses for the prisoners' daughters. Many POWs in the early days of American involvement in the war had no love for Hitler, and they were grateful for their capture. The government paid them wages if they worked, and many prisoners held at Camp Concordia went to movies and took University of Kansas extension courses. My dad and his brothers even drafted the men working on the Kuhlmann farm to play baseball with them and their friends until my Uncle Dale accidentally beaned a prisoner in the head with an errant pitch, knocking him unconscious. Grandma insisted that the Germans refrain from playing anymore with the boys for fear the men would get hurt.

Many German POWs from Camp Concordia had such fondness for their time of captivity that hundreds of them returned to Kansas for prison camp reunions after the war. Those captured late in the war, however, were the real deal Nazis—malicious young men who had swallowed whole Hitler's doctrine of hate. My dad remembered one teenaged prisoner who enjoyed lecturing my grandfather about Germany's inevitable victory. One day, the kid purposely cut down several rows of immature corn. When grandpa called him on it, the young detainee started screaming.

"Sehr bald werden unsere Flugzeuge den Himmel füllen und Sie alle werden sterben!" (Very soon, our airplanes will fill the skies, and you will all die!) Grandpa requested that Camp Concordia find another work opportunity for this prisoner.

By the way, I'm not suggesting that the earlier prisoners were not complicit in the horror that was the Third Reich. Millions of good people were caught up in the Nazi juggernaut, but we all have a duty to stand for what is right and to repel what is not. The good people of Germany failed to do that. Edmund Burke, anyone?

In the fall of 1943, an itinerant handyman began working at the farm. His name was Bill Smith, and he performed mechanical and building repairs during the day and made an occasional errand run to town. He, too, ate dinner with the family, and he slept in the barn where in his spare time he listened to his shortwave radio. Sometimes he let my dad listen to war news with him. During the spring of 1944, Bill's trips to town became more frequent, but no one paid much attention. One early June evening, Dad was listening to the radio with Bill, who was unusually agitated.

"*Ve* vill vin, Marfin!" Bill exclaimed. "*Ve* vill vin!" Up to this point, Bill had spoken with a generic American accent.

My dad suddenly realized the handyman was not what he seemed. Allied forces landed on the beaches of Normandy a few days later, and "Bill" went to town on an errand and never returned.

Dad and his siblings attended St. John Lutheran School, known locally as the German School, through eighth grade. It was a one-room affair, and most of the students were related to each other. It must have been a decent school because my dad could compute six-digit long division problems in his head better than I can on paper, and he could do so as quickly as I'm able to do with a calculator. By eighth grade graduation, St. John students were also conversant in Shakespeare, Blake, Homer, and Goethe.

Following elementary school, Dad attended Chester High School where he lettered in track and basketball, and, as a junior, played the romantic lead in the play *The Jade Ring*. He was junior class vice president, senior class president, and the senior reporter for *The Bulldog's Tale*, the school yearbook. Something of a try-hard, as my son would say.

School assemblies at Chester High consisted of pep rallies for the six-man football team or the appearance of a local farmer who showed up each month in his work overalls to recite the poetry of James Whitcomb Riley.

"Didn't you think that was totally stupid?" I asked my dad when I was a teenager.

"No," he said. "We all loved it when he came to school."

I couldn't get my head around that. It sounded like the most boring thing ever.

"I was a yokel with no electricity or indoor plumbing," my dad said. "It impressed me that this guy had memorized all those poems." Then I had to sit and listen to my dad recite "Out to Old Aunt Mary's," which failed to enchant me because I had indoor plumbing *and* television.

❧

On a back page of the 1949 edition of *The Bulldog's Tale*, an ad for the local Methodist church touts it as "the friendly church"[1]—a pointed statement considering that the only other church in town was the Lutheran congregation. Unfortunately, the ad was dead-on.

When my dad was a child attending St. John Lutheran Church, men and women were required to sit on opposite sides of the sanctuary, presumably so no one would have impure thoughts, even about their spouse, during the service. Having known many of them, I have a hard time imagining those austere Germans engaging in lustful fantasies at all, let alone in church. Thoughts of hog prices, maybe. Sex, not so much. Children were obliged to sit in the first two rows—gender-appropriate sides, of course.

Dad and his brothers were required to attend both early and late worship every Sunday. Their parents made them walk the two miles to town for the early English language service, followed by Sunday school. My grandparents attended the later German service and mandated that the boys stay for that one, too, because "it was good for them."

It's no shock to any twenty-first century parent that the three boys, bored and sick to death of church, made the mistake one interminable morning of looking through their Sunday school handouts during sermon number two. No big deal, right? This doesn't even rise to the "hand them some Cheerios or drawing paper" level of behavior. But this was 1937 at the decidedly unfriendly Lutheran church.

Angry that the three boys were paying more attention to their Bible story papers than to the sermon, the pastor stopped preaching and, from the pulpit, screamed at them, berating them and warning them that such behavior gone unchecked would lead them straight to Hell. How dare they disrupt a sacred occasion with such folly? The diatribe would have been bad enough if the pastor had ranted in English, but he shouted at them in German, a language in which even kind words sound harsh. Grace, mercy, and peace, indeed.

Let's admit that church can be really boring for children. When I was a kid in Flint, Michigan, I used to dread the Sundays when my dad was out of town for a conference or speaking engagement because in his absence Pastor Becker, a truly decent man who excelled at ministering to the sick and lonely in Flint's nursing homes, filled the pulpit. He was the worst public speaker I've ever heard.

He mumbled his sermon and rustled his heavily relied-upon notes so loudly that the ineffective pulpit microphone picked up only the sound of crunching paper. Once, during a prolonged sermon of his, I opened a hymnal and started leafing through it. It wasn't twenty seconds before my mom gave me a look that could kill, took the book from me, dramatically closed it, and put it back in the slot on the pew back. No one was going to accuse *this* pastor's wife of having an unruly child! Mom was in lecture mode later that day, but I wasn't backing down.

"He's terrible!" I argued. "I can't hear him most of the time, and when I can, he's boring!"

My mom had her rebuttal ready. "He's not why you are there listening and learning, young lady. Your Savior is. It won't kill you to listen respectfully for twenty minutes."

Except she didn't say that. Instead, she told me, "His daughter Joyce plays for Andre Previn in the Pittsburgh Symphony Orchestra, Karen Ann."

With logic like that, how could I not listen, enraptured, to Pastor Becker?

❧

If the pastor in Chester was uncompromising during church services, it was in confirmation instruction that he really played hardball. In the Lutheran Church-Missouri Synod, children generally are confirmed in the faith near the end of eighth grade. They take classes from their pastor for two years, memorizing *Luther's Small Catechism* and learning Christian and Lutheran doctrine. Upon completion of instruction, the students, or confirmands as they are commonly called, affirm during a church service the Holy Spirit's gift of faith given them at their respective baptisms in infancy. When my parents were kids, babies didn't leave the house until the buggy ride to church for Holy Baptism—never more than two Sundays following the birth. Today, most Lutheran babies make it to Target and Chili's before they are baptized. Too often, getting grandmas and grandpas and aunts and uncles to town for the occasion is seen as more important than the rite itself. My husband and I waited a month for our son's baptism for the same reason. I was the guilty party. Jim, a former Baptist, accurately pointed out the irony of Lutherans preaching about the importance of infant baptism, yet sometimes waiting months to make it happen.

My dad began confirmation instruction in 1943, his seventh-grade year. He attended with kids he had known since first grade. The pastor arrived at exactly 9:00 a.m. that first Saturday morning and was for the next two years never more than thirty seconds early or one second late.

"He never once in two years smiled," Dad told me. "He said confirmation class was no place for happiness."

Herr Pastor Neuhaus did not tolerate absences, informing the students that missing class was one of the grossest sins, ranking right up there with sin against the Holy Spirit. Every session was a lecture about Heaven and Hell, with special emphasis on Hell. The morning began with a hymn followed by a Bible reading which, no matter the verse, the pastor related to Hell. Psalm 23:1, "The Lord is my shepherd; I shall not want." Hell. Philippians 4:13, "I can do all things through Christ who strengthens me." Hell. The kids were drilled in the Ten Commandments, which gave the pastor ample opportunity to discuss each student's inevitable march toward damnation. Finally, there was memory work—the time set aside for the perfect recitation of Lutheran doctrine and the scripture verse used to reinforce it. My dad hated memory work time—not because he wasn't prepared, but because of what happened to Donnie Elwell.

Donnie, a town kid, spent Saturday afternoons at the farm catching pigeons in the barn. My dad didn't like heights, so it was Don's job to grab the hay rope and climb thirty feet up to the point of the pulley in the center of the roof peak. At the pulley, the rope ran parallel with the peak of the barn roof and the floor below. Hand over hand, Don moved along the rope, forty-five feet to the cupola into which he flung himself feet first. He snatched the roosting pigeons, locking their wings over their backs, and tossed them to my dad. Don then reversed the process, lowered himself to the barn floor, and took the pigeons home to his mother, who was grateful for the extra food.

"He never dared me to make the climb," Dad told me. "And he didn't call me a chicken for not volunteering to take a turn."

Confirmation class, however, did not come easily to Don, where he struggled with memory work. On the day each student was required to stand individually and recite Part III of The Sacrament of Holy Baptism from *Luther's Small Catechism*, Don began with confidence but quickly lost his way.

"How can water do such great things? It is not the water indeed that does them—"[2] He stopped, unable to recall the rest. The pastor yelled at Don for laziness, insolence, and general sinfulness, but stopped short of issuing a rabbit punch, his favorite method of keeping the boys in line. Instead, he belittled Don for what was his worst fault.

"Oh, yes," the pastor said with a sneer. "Your father is a Methodist."

My dad sat there, tense and angry.

"I didn't say anything," Dad told me. "I wanted to tell the pastor that he wouldn't say that to Don if he could see him on the rope in our barn. But I was young and scared, so I said nothing."

The students were confirmed on April 29, 1945—one day before Hitler took his own life in a Berlin bunker. Radio stations were already announcing plans for VE and VJ Day celebrations as my dad and Donnie made their vows to be faithful to Christ unto death.

Dad had, by this time, decided to become a pastor. He felt called to serve God; but did he also, looking at the parade of stern and sometimes cruel men in the pulpit, think, "I can do a better job than this"?

After high school graduation, my dad saw his old confirmation instructor one more time. On school break from the seminary, Dad was invited to preach the sermon at his home congregation. As the service was starting, he saw the former pastor, now broken down by age and infirmity, enter the sanctuary. My dad was a stellar preacher even then, but he readily admitted that his sermon that day was a sterile piece of writing prepared for the classroom—cold, clinical, and without soul. After the service,

Dad went to the door to greet people as they left. When Pastor Neuhaus walked by, he didn't speak but smiled at my dad for the first time.

"Do you think that meant he was proud of you?" I asked.

My dad replied, "I think it meant 'Good luck, buddy. You're gonna need it.'"

Do I really want to live in Chester, Nebraska? Sometimes I think I do, especially since the Lutheran congregation now competes with the Methodist church in friendliness. Would I be happy there? Probably, but only if I looked at the town through the prism of my childhood and the stories from my dad's upbringing. That would mean living in the past, however, which my parents taught me not to do. When my cousin Karla posts on Facebook about harvest and winning ribbons for her pies at the county fair, I'm envious of the significance of community and shared purpose of the people who work hard to supply our suburban superstores with food. Sometimes the anonymity that comes with living in a city means that, except for church, I can go weeks without running into a friend or an acquaintance. How great would it be to address my grocery checker or my bank teller by name? What would it be like to walk into a restaurant and know everyone well enough to lose track of time chatting? I come to my senses, though, when I remember that unless you've spent your entire life in a small town, you're an outsider. Besides, they don't have Google Fiber.

If I'm honest, I'm glad I don't live in Chester, but I'm thankful my dad did because his time there, and the people, made him who he was—a tough, optimistic man with an unshakeable faith in his Savior. The hard work of the prairie gave my dad poetry for the pulpit, and he never forgot where he came from, where he was going, or to Whom he belonged.

Chapter Three

A Heavy Weight on Tiny Shoulders

Mom (far right, front row)
with her family, 1942

My mom, Donna, grew up in Denison, Iowa, a small agricultural town in the west central part of the state. The town was a metropolis compared to Chester. Because most of my relatives moved away from Denison before I was born, we made only rare and, for me, excruciating visits to see my mom's grandmother, who was a stranger to me. My great-grandmother, Cena, was so foreign that she frightened me and made my German relations in Chester look baseball-and-apple-pie American in comparison. Cena's thick accent rendered her English indecipherable, she was balding and missing most of her teeth, and she watched television with a shotgun resting across her lap. Whenever we paid an afternoon visit, she hobbled around on one crutch, dressed in her flowered housecoat and bulky gray sweater, setting out food for my parents and me. I sat in the hot, dark room (all my relatives were big on keeping the curtains drawn and the lights off) silently praying we would leave soon. God ignored me.

"Isn't your girl going to eat?" Cena asked my mom, gesturing to my untouched food. It irritated me how all my foreign-born family never referred to children by their proper names. "The Girl" was also how Cena referred to the mentally-challenged young woman from town who came to help with chores.

"Karen Ann," my mom prodded, "eat something!"

The afternoon snack consisted of pickled herring, Limburger cheese from an old mayonnaise jar on the kitchen counter, liver-wurst, and hard brown bread. I mouthed "no" as inconspicuously as I could, and Mom dissembled, saying I wasn't hungry.

The other person present at our get-togethers with Cena was Henry, a man I assumed was my great-grandfather and referred to him as such during one visit. My mom swiftly hushed me. What was the deal? He clearly lived there, but I noticed that my mom called him by his first name. Was he a step-grandfather she resented?

"So, what *is* Henry to you?" I asked her the second we backed out of Cena's driveway.

"Never mind, Karen Ann," she said.

"Why never mind?" I asked. "He must be something to you."

"I'm done talking about this," she answered, so I dropped it. It wasn't until I was a teenager that I figured out Cena and Henry were shacking up. Given their advanced ages, there was probably considerably more friendship than benefits involved, but the arrangement embarrassed my mom. I hate that Mom always felt guilty and responsible for situations in which she had no part and over which she had no control. I don't much care for it when I do the same thing.

I had no real ties to Denison except a tenuous one concerning the town's most famous daughter—Donna Reed. My mom was twelve years younger than Ms. Reed and closer in age to the star's younger sister, Karen, with whom Mom attended high school. Donna Reed already was a Hollywood star, and her perennially well-dressed and well-coiffed sister could have been stuck up about it—especially toward my mom, who was too poor to be well-anything. But Karen Mullenger (Reed was a stage name) was warm and friendly, and she won Mom's admiration, her respect, and a love of the name Karen.

❦

My mom's childhood was not as easy as my dad's. She dealt as a young girl with some tough things: guilt, poverty, and law minus grace at church. When I was ten, I discovered the primary source of her guilt. I was rooting around in my dad's desk for some paper and came across my parents' baptismal certificates. Both were beautifully illustrated and filled out in authoritative German script. I noticed that my mom's birth year was listed as 1934 instead of the correct 1933, so I took the certificate to her and pointed out the mistake. I also noted that her parents' marriage date must have been erroneously recorded since it predated her actual birthday by only six months.

Mom's face crimsoned, and she ordered me to put the certificate back where I had found it. She ignored me when I asked what was wrong. It finally dawned on me a couple of years later that my Schneller grandparents' wedding had been of the shotgun variety. The pastor who filled out the certificate had, either by accident or intent, "legitimized" my mother's birth. I wisely waited a few years to ask Mom about it, and she admitted that her parents were "two people who should not have married each other." I have no doubt that my grandparents were committed to their marriage—they were from a generation that stuck things out in good times and in bad. My grandpa, a barroom brawler in his youth, gentled in old age, so I only knew him as a cute old man dressed in steel gray work clothes who drank coffee from a saucer and ended meals with a stick of Doublemint gum. Grandma was large and loud, and, although she was never unkind to me, I knew I wasn't a favorite among her fourteen grandchildren.

I rarely witnessed tenderness between Mom's parents, but there must have been a spark when they were young because, by their sixth anniversary, they had three children. My grandparents enjoyed going dancing in town on Friday nights, and they tasked my mom with watching her younger siblings, Wayne and Arlene, in their absence. Mom was five years old when her mother and father first left her to care for her toddler brother and infant sister—while they went out and had fun. The late-night noises of the house and yard scared her as she waited for her parents' return.

"Weren't you afraid of somebody breaking in?" I asked her before recalling that they never locked their doors, making it unnecessary for any potential thief, rapist, or murderer to break anything.

"No, but I was terrified there would be a fire, and I wouldn't be strong or fast enough to put it out," she told me. "I knew my parents would blame me if something happened to my brother and sister."

A part of me resents my grandparents for their carefree indulgence at the expense of their daughter's safety, peace of mind, and childhood. Mom was also, at age five, responsible for driving their cattle from pasture to pasture, without supervision, along a busy stretch of highway. I can't help but see this through my own prism of motherhood, and it makes me queasy to think of the possibly tragic outcomes. My mom was a witty lady with a wonderful sense of irony, but she never once in her life let down her guard. Now that I'm a parent and make my share of mistakes, I'm more understanding of my grandparents. I will never *not* think that placing their child in such precarious and unsuitable (these days criminally negligent) situations was the height of selfishness and lunacy, but parenthood might be the role that reveals the most chinks in our armor—and provides the clearest evidence that much of what we do in life requires the forgiveness of a loving God.

Most people assume that my dad, because he was a pastor, was the more stridently Lutheran of my parents; but, in fact, he wore his Lutheran-ness comfortably while my mom worked hard to fit in and prove her bona fides.

My Grandma Schneller (which in German means "faster") was solidly Lutheran, but my grandpa was a lapsed Catholic when they married. One set of his grandparents were Jews who had escaped persecution in Russia. They settled in Bavaria, where they converted to Catholicism. As blond and fair as the Kuhlmanns were, my Schneller relations were dark and olive-skinned. An old photo from my dad's first visit to Mom's family looks like some Nordic guy popped in on the Sicilian set of *The Godfather*.

Grandpa Schneller became Lutheran after marriage but still adhered to the practice of no meat on Fridays, and, still uncomfortable with his new denomination, didn't take his young family to church. He did agree to send my mom and her siblings to Zion Lutheran School, where, as members, they attended tuition-free. My mom craved the opportunity to learn, but she didn't like Zion. Some things never change—it's hard to fit in when people zero in on your poverty. As much as Jesus admonishes his followers to care for the poor, we sometimes reserve our love and compassion for people who have nothing while we look with disdain on people who have enough to get by but not enough to dress well.

Mom's family didn't weather the Depression as easily as did my dad's. Grandpa Schneller worked hard, but he hadn't been gifted a debt-free farm. Instead, he farmed rented properties and often left town for Works Progress Administration jobs where he labored on a road crew and earned 36¢ per day—a wage my mom emphasized to me when I complained about my low-paying teenage jobs.

Money in the Schneller household was for food and shelter. Clothing came from the poor barrel at church, and, unluckily for my mom, she always ended up with the pastor's daughters' castoffs. On Mondays, the school day Mom dreaded most, the girls let everyone know about it.

First on the class agenda for the week was the public taking of church attendance. After the teacher called each student's name, that child was required to stand and say "yes" or "no" when asked if they had been in church the preceding day. All the students except my mom answered in the affirmative. She was humiliated every week because her answer was always "no." As she stood watching her teacher lower her religion grade in the class ledger and listening to him rebuke her for not caring enough about Jesus to get to church, the pastor's daughters, mean girls to the core, made fun of Mom for wearing their old dresses. This was when my mother first believed that she would never be good enough, or Lutheran enough, and that God must be terribly disappointed in her.

Following her time at Zion Lutheran School, Mom attended Denison High School, where, according to the signings in her yearbook, she excelled at gym, home economics, and, shocking to me because she regularly belittled herself for a self-perceived lack of intelligence, biology. One classmate chastises her for setting the curve too high, and several thank her for allowing them to copy her notes. Another student thanks her for letting him cheat off her paper during tests, which makes me feel better about cheating on a chemistry quiz during my junior year of high school. The yearbook also reveals intriguing comments about the fist fights that regularly erupted during literature class, in which my mom did not take part but which entertained her, nonetheless. Her senior class trip was a picnic at a state park about ninety miles east of Denison—the name of which caused a long and ridiculous misunderstanding between us.

My senior class trip was a cruise to The Bahamas. I had no desire to go because I knew what (and who) was going to go down once the ship left port. Also, there was no way my parents were going to spring for two grand to cover the trip's expenses. Mom could not let go of the fact that the senior trip was a cruise. Again, I didn't want to go, didn't ask to go, and didn't complain that I was not going. But I made the critical mistake of mentioning, in passing, the trip.

"What do you mean, Karen Ann?" my mom demanded. "A cruise? For high schoolers? That's *ridiculous!*"

"Technically, they aren't high schoolers anymore," I answered.

"Well, you can put *that* idea out of your head right now, young lady!"

"It's not in my head!"

"Well, you are not going!"

"I never said I wanted to go!"

"Do you know where I went on *my* senior trip?" she asked. "Do you?"

"How would I know that?"

"We went to Legis State Park and had a picnic. And it was fun!" According to Verna Stolz's note in my mom's yearbook, it was "wild."

"Legis State Park? What kind of stupid name is that?"

"It was a wonderful park!"

"Was it named after judges or lawyers or something?" I asked. "That is so stupid."

"Where on earth would you get *that* idea?"

Following this conversation, I made fun of Legis State Park and my mother whenever she reminisced about it. I had no reason to do so other than I was young and thought I knew everything. Several years later, I looked at a map, and there it was—*Ledges* State Park. If you say it out loud, it's easy to understand my mistake, but I'm an idiot just the same.

Mom's ambition was to attend college and study library science, but her parents wouldn't allow it. They didn't believe in higher education for a man, let alone a woman. This was still true when I went to college. I remember sitting in a circle of lawn chairs outside my grandparents' house on a hot July evening as my parents talked about how they would have to adjust to me leaving home in a few weeks for my freshman year at Northwest Missouri State University.

"There's no reason for girls to go to college," Grandma Schneller declared. "I don't even know why people spend money for boys to go."

Mom had to put up a hell of a fight to get her parents' permission and a bit of their money to go to college. They acquiesced with the stipulation that she had to become a teacher—the only acceptable profession, in their opinion, for a woman. Mom also had to attend a Lutheran school and remain single for life because they believed all teachers should be unmarried. My grandparents could not have predicted that my mom, on her first day at St. John's College in Winfield, Kansas, would meet my dad in the campus bookstore and start dating him that week, foiling their plans for her spinsterhood and altering my dad's path to the ministry.

Chapter Four

Beginnings of a Wonderful Life

Mom and Dad, 1953

The Lutheran Church-Missouri Synod takes the education of its pastors seriously. Guys with a desire to minister can't announce, "Hey, everybody, I'm a pastor now," and immediately start preaching, as is the case in some denominations. I'm not aware of the current requirements for seminary students in the LCMS, but my dad had to earn Bachelor of Arts and Bachelor of Divinity degrees. He also graduated with a Master of Divinity degree, but I'm not certain that was compulsory for the ministry.

Before entering Concordia Theological Seminary in St. Louis, Dad attended St. John's College in Winfield, Kansas, a two-year college with an affiliated high school preparatory academy. He arrived in 1949 for a three-year stint, an extra year required for him because Chester High School didn't offer Greek, a language in which he'd have to demonstrate at least some proficiency before enrolling at the seminary.

Dad's first two years at St. John's were typical for a young man at a Lutheran college. He ran track, studied Greek, joined Polyhymnia Choir, pledged a literary society, studied more Greek, and mailed his laundry home weekly so his mother could wash it and send it back to him (okay, maybe that wasn't so typical). Missouri Synod colleges don't have traditional fraternities and sororities, so literary societies provided opportunities for fun and service. The two most popular societies for male students at St. John's were Chrysostomos, known as Chrys (pronounced "cries"), and Demosthenian, whose members were known as Demons. Chrys, according to *The Johnnie* yearbook, excelled in forensics, enjoyed picnics, and were known for their sportsmanship during intramural athletic contests. The Demosthenian group had a reputation for dominating the intramural football and basketball leagues and throwing parties for the girls' societies. Their most infamous bash, which they hosted for the girls of Delta Alpha Kappa Society, was the Demon Den of Horror.[1] It does not surprise me at all that my dad opted to be a Demon.

Dad was intent on several things during his final year at St. John's—passing all his classes, beating the Chrys into submission on the basketball court, and getting started on the road to the ministry. But he hadn't counted on getting serious about a girl, because Concordia Seminary was dead serious about its rule that ministerial students could not be married until after graduation.

During the first year that my parents dated, Dad continued as a Demon, and Mom joined the Deltas who, according to the yearbook, went on hikes, hosted the Demon-Delta Valentine party, and made Easter baskets for residents of the local children's home.[2] Mom and her roommate, Dee, took up smoking and attempted to hide their habit from the dorm matron, spinsterly Miss Dietrich, by whom they were busted on several occasions. The rug they stuffed under their door may have adequately kept the smoke from wafting into the hallway, but they had not counted on Miss Dietrich making a nightly walk around the building to see which girls were violating "lights out" at 10:00 p.m. Mom and Dee pulled weekend cleaning duty whenever they accrued too many demerits.

"Demerits?" I was amazed when I found out about this. "When did you go to college—1875?" I was equally shocked at the early bedtime required for people in their late teens and early twenties.

My dad had a fairly clean slate in college—he probably was better than my mom at avoiding detection when he decided to flout the rules. He got into real trouble, however, when Miss Dietrich caught him with his arm around my mom's shoulder as they sat together on a couch in the dorm lounge. This breach of the strict "no touching" mandate resulted in the month-long impoundment of my dad's car. Based on the signings in Mom's yearbook, this punishment cut into their Friday night make-out sessions during which they and their companions drank a disgusting combination of Coke and sloe gin.

My parents were already talking about marriage when my dad graduated from St. John's, and yearbook notes from my mom's friends tell of her sadness at having to wait five years before she and my dad could marry. I'm glad I didn't read the notations until recently. Had I seen them when I was a child or teenager, I would have felt like throwing up at the entries that encouraged my parents to "have fun making curly-haired babies."

They held out fewer than two years. Mom had graduated from St. John's in 1953 and was teaching in Litchfield, Illinois. Dad had completed one year of seminary when they eloped, deciding they didn't want to wait any longer and that, eventually, the unsustainable seminary rule would have to change if the LCMS wanted to continue to attract young men to the ministry. My dad never regretted the choice to put his ministry on hold. In fact, my brother and I often talk about how it probably made him a better pastor.

When Dad died, Brent and I set up the requisite memorabilia table for the visitation, and we included his seminary transcripts. He aced Hebrew, homiletics, dogmatics, field work, and the lively-sounding Eisenach Old Testament selections. The classes in which he did a more mediocre job were biblical theology, Old Testament exegesis, the Church in the Roman Empire, Isaiah, Romans, Jeremiah, and the doctrine of justification by faith. A local pastor who graduated from St. John's with my dad, and who waited to marry, approached me at the funeral dinner to talk about Dad's report card.

"I forgot until now that Marv left the seminary for a few years," Pastor Ludwig said. "I saw his grades—couldn't hack it, huh?" Mr. Goody Two-shoes Good Grades wasn't joking.

My dad's grades for his last couple of years at the seminary were not his best, but he earned them while married and parenting a young son. He was taking a full schedule of classes by day and, in addition to studying and spending scant time with his family, worked at Schnucks Grocery Store to earn extra cash. Pastor Ludwig had picked the wrong time to be cute.

"My dad, I believe you know, left school because he didn't want to wait to marry my mom," I told him. "And it's clear those grades don't tell the whole story."

During the six years that my dad waited for the policy change at the seminary, he and my mom settled in Centralia, Missouri, where her family had moved from Denison, Iowa. Centralia seems an unlikely choice to me, mainly because my Schneller grandparents, still adamant that teachers should remain unmarried, were furious at my mom for ignoring their wishes. They got over their anger, though, because they adored my dad. In fact, it was clear to me growing up that Dad was closer to my mom's family than he was to his own.

The Kuhlmann side of the family was quiet, reserved, and polite to each other. My brother and I find it hilarious that our Grandma Kuhlmann greeted us with handshakes rather than hugs. The Schnellers, on the other hand, were loud, demonstrative, and sometimes argumentative. They also drank more. I had my first drink of Old Crow bourbon whiskey as a five-year-old when Grandpa Schneller passed a bottle to us younger cousins while we sat around the kitchen table learning from him how to play Pitch.

An introverted child, I was never comfortable around my mom's family. They were never mean to me, but, unlike my brother, I wasn't one of them. When Dad was ordained, Brent was almost ten years old and had grown up with our Schneller cousins, aunts, uncles, and grandparents. His connection to our Grandma Schneller was a particularly tender one. She babysat him while Mom taught school and Dad worked at a brick plant in the intervening years before returning to the seminary. Brent has always credited Grandma Schneller as a primary spiritual influence in his life. At his confirmation service, when he was a thirteen-year-old in Liberty, Missouri, Grandma stopped to cradle Brent's face in her hands as she filed past the line of kids who had been confirmed a few moments earlier.

"Remember this," she told him. Brent has never forgotten the impact of those simple but emphatic words she spoke with love and conviction. I won't pretend I was ever close to Grandma Schneller, but it was clear that her faith was strong and sincere.

Brent is the oldest among the Schneller cousins, and I am nearly the youngest. Over the years, age differences and distance combined to make me feel like an outsider. Of course, my mom's unflagging lectures about the proper way for a pastor's child to behave made it impossible for me to relax. If I had been able to loosen up, I might have learned to enjoy her family more than I did. Additionally, I was judgmental of my mom's side of the family, and I should not have been. Ideally, we all go through a tenderizing process as we get older and find out that life isn't easy or fair and that we all are, as my dad often reminded me, beggars in search of bread. Now that we're adults with children and, in some cases, grandchildren, and we rarely see each other except at funerals, I'd love to sit around a table and connect with my cousins over a few beers or a bottle of Old Crow.

The Schneller cousins that I know best, but not well, are my Uncle Wayne's kids—Sterling, Valerie, and Connie. (Their younger brother, Greg, died a couple of years ago.) We don't often get opportunities to visit, but the reminiscence of a shared childhood incident is always a guaranteed icebreaker.

I was six years old when my parents, Brent, and I traveled the 150 miles from the parsonage in Liberty, Missouri, to Centralia for an overnight visit. I don't remember the time of year, but that Sunday afternoon was chilly when most of the extended family gathered at the farm. Everybody was going about their business. Some of us kids were playing board games while others were outside with Hud, the exuberant farm dog that terrified me. Grandma, Mom, and the aunts were preparing food, and my dad and the uncles had wandered off somewhere. At some point, my Aunt Arlene noticed that it had been awhile since she had seen her seven-year-old son, Kevin. The adults checked the house, yard, and outbuildings for Kevin, to no avail. After forty minutes of fruitless searching, their attention turned to a collapsed and, at the time, flooded underground storage cave on the property. Everyone was certain Kevin had fallen into the cave. Grandpa grabbed a shovel, stripped to his undershirt, and dug around in the mud and water while the women clung to each other and wept. Brent and Sterling, who were fifteen and fourteen respectively, assumed Kevin was dead. Because they had been told to watch the younger kids, they were convinced they would be blamed for Kevin's demise. Panicked and crying, they fled to the pasture to recite the Lord's Prayer.

After half an hour watching Grandpa stir the murky cave water, a few of us younger cousins grew tired of waiting for Kevin's body to surface, so we went inside to get a drink from the communal water pail and dipper. Minutes later, my dad and uncles returned from a trip to the local pool hall—with Kevin, whom they had taken to town without informing anyone.

"You're in big trouble," we taunted Kevin. We were wrong.

At lunch that evening ("lunch" is what my German relatives called the second supper served around 8:00 p.m.), the women served ham, rye bread, brown mustard, lemon gelatin salad with marshmallows, and chocolate cream pie. All the men except Grandpa received extra helpings of tight-lipped blame. Kevin was treated like a king—until he dropped his plate of food on the avocado-green living room carpet. All the good will he had earned by being presumed dead was gone. Momentary clumsiness, dirtying the carpet, and wasting perfectly good food added up to the trifecta of shame for a kid with fastidious German relatives. The aunts grudgingly offered him a second plate of food and carried it to the table for him so "he wouldn't make another mess." Kevin didn't touch a bite.

❧

Concordia Seminary finally changed its rule on the marriage issue, so my parents left Centralia and Mom's family, and Dad resumed his studies in the fall of 1960. Dad, Mom, and Brent lived in a top floor walk-up apartment on Lansdowne Avenue in St. Louis. I envied my parents and brother when they shared memories of stifling heat in the summer and neighbors who washed their stoops each morning. It sounded like something out of *A Tree Grows in Brooklyn,* and I begrudged them a life of exoticism that didn't include me.

Dad graduated in May 1963. "Call Day," when students receive their initial congregational placements, occurred a week prior to graduation and was, arguably, the bigger deal. Once a pastor has served at a congregation, he has the choice to accept a call to either serve another parish or remain where he is. Although graduating students have input about geographical preferences, they have no say about which congregation they will serve right out of the seminary.

Dad was one of the older graduates in 1963, and he had proven himself so useful as a vicar (a pastoral intern) at St. Matthew Lutheran Church in St. Louis that the congregation, which had a pastoral vacancy at the time, requested him for an extra year. During Dad's two-year vicarage, he was de facto pastor of the thousand-member congregation. Prior to ordination, he couldn't perform weddings, but he could baptize, confirm, and bury. Dad's other duties, as specified in his vicarage agreement, were shut-in calls, hospital calls, home sick visits "of a sufficient number," youth counseling, delinquent member visits, preaching, youth vespers, confirmation instruction, weekly Sunday school teachers' meetings (it's almost impossible to get Sunday school teachers to meet *quarterly* now), youth Bible classes, and regular forays into the surrounding area to visit the four hundred unchurched families that lived within a mile of the church. It's no wonder that, in later years, Dad had zero patience for lazy vicars.

Because Dad had more practical experience than his fellow graduates, and because the powers that be told him he was the only one who could handle the downside of it, the seminary assigned him to be the pastor of St. Peter Lutheran Church in Westgate, Iowa—a farming community with about 200 inhabitants. The congregation, drawing from the unincorporated countryside, had 350 members.

The drawback to St. Peter Lutheran, and the reason my dad was handpicked to be their pastor, was that in 1963 it was one of the lowest-paying congregations in the Missouri Synod. Dad had earned, per his vicarage contract, $250 per month in 1962. His salary for his first year in the ministry would not increase, and there would be another mouth to feed. Dad was ordained into the ministry on June 30, 1963, and I was born nine months later. I once asked my mom if they had held off having another child until my dad was done with school.

"You were our little ordination celebration, Karen Ann!" Mom said.

"Please stop," I begged. "Forget I even asked."

When Dad began his ministry in Westgate, he continued his real, practical education. Dealing with sick and dying people, for example, takes practice—they don't teach Congregants' Benign Tumors in a Jar 101 at the seminary. My dad had no problem later in his ministry when, during hospital visits, people showed him their incisions or souvenir gallstones, but on his first hospital call as a vicar he had to excuse himself to throw up during a parishioner's grisly post-op play-by-play.

Classroom instruction also can't adequately prepare people for low salaries, gossip, double standards for ministers' families versus everyone else, or the huge amount of time a pastor spends away from his wife and kids. But Dad was always quick to say that the benefits of his calling, both tangible and intangible, far outweighed the inconveniences. He entered the ministry armed, certainly, with God's grace, but also with diligence and a positive attitude. My mom, despite her insecurities, was made of stern stuff, and she was Dad's best asset. Her insistence on perfect behavior from Brent and me probably made Dad's ministry easier for her, although it made our childhoods more stressful. We received regular lectures during our childhood and teen years about irresponsible conduct that we must never engage in—everything from slouching in church to using drugs, both of which were equally unpardonable for a pastor's children. But Mom never insisted that our dad cancel meetings to be home with her, she wasn't a gossip, and she never complained to people about how challenging it was to be a pastor's wife.

Our lives as a pastor's family began in rural Iowa during a kind of Golden Age to be a kid and to be a Lutheran—although the time in Westgate would test my parents' abilities to put food on the table. Just as the circumstances of my parents' childhoods formed them, the next twenty years and four congregations would shape me for better and for worse. My brother knew our dad as a laborer in a brick plant, a grocery store bagger, and a student. Brent sat with both parents in church for much of his upbringing, while I found it weird and slightly unnerving when Dad sat with us on Sundays during vacations. I have never known anything different than being a pastor's kid. It hasn't always been easy—moving around and trying to form relationships is tough for an introvert like me—but I've also experienced inordinate amounts of love and generosity. The people and congregations my dad ministered to haven't been perfect, but neither was our family. My mom had the hardest role—being a pastor's wife is not easy—but she persevered, and most of the time we managed to laugh at each other and ourselves. So, apropos for me, named after Donna Reed's sister, it truly has been a wonderful life.

Chapter Five

Poor and Hungry

St. Peter Lutheran Church steeple,
Westgate, Iowa

My teenage son eats a lot. He's a rock-solid six feet, two inches tall and weighs 190 pounds. Once, after a nasty bout of flu, he celebrated his return to good health by eating a bag of Sun Chips and half a bag of Fudge Stripe cookies before getting a double cheeseburger, fries, and shake from Freddy's. This snack and meal set me back seventeen dollars. When my parents, my brother, and I lived in Westgate, Iowa, their typical dinner for two adults and one pre-teen was a box of Kraft macaroni and cheese and a bowl of iceberg lettuce with sliced tomatoes. Presumably, I had baby formula and a few scraps of macaroni. That meal cost less than one dollar—a good thing because we were living below the poverty line.

Two hundred and fifty dollars a month didn't go far, even in the early 1960s. If you figure correctly that my mom squeezed the life out of every dime my dad earned, they probably spent about three dollars a day on food. My dad made $3,000 a year, before taxes, at St. Peter Lutheran Church, a salary which cbsnews.com indicates was at least twenty-five percent less than the $4,400 the average American earned that year.[1] We lived in church housing, so there was no mortgage payment, and the parsonage in Westgate was huge—two stories with a full attic, five bedrooms, study, living room, dining room, kitchen, and two bathrooms. Years later, my mom wore a dreamy look whenever she described the house, which she said had more character than all the other parsonages we lived in combined. "The things I could do with that place now," she sighed. "It's too bad that what we want and what we need don't always happen at the same time."

What my parents needed in Westgate was a house that didn't cost so much to heat. They were on the hook for parsonage utilities, and the inefficient oil furnace burned a copious amount of expensive fuel during the long northern Iowa winters. The light bill wasn't cheap, either, and one member of the congregation's Board of Elders was a continual source of frustration for my parents as they tried to keep costs down. The church owned a portable marquee-type sign that advertised church service times, and every evening this guy drove to the church property and plugged it into the parsonage outlet, not wanting the congregation to pay for the electricity. After the church elder climbed back in his car and motored home, Dad went outside and pulled the plug.

The pastor who preceded my dad at St. Peter Lutheran ministered there for thirty years without a bump in pay. He and his wife had five children, and they raised livestock on the church grounds for food and extra income. Prior to my parents' move-in date, the St. Peter Board of Trustees razed the barn adjacent to the parsonage, supposing correctly that the new pastor had no desire to undertake a little animal husbandry on the side.

Soon after their arrival in Westgate, my parents and brother drove to Rochester, Minnesota, to take advantage of a furniture sale. They purchased dining, living room, and bedroom sets, and a desk for my dad—all for $300. Some of the pieces lacked quality. The bed frame and dresser that I used until I left for college were plywood covered with gray paint, but the gorgeous mid-century modern dining table and china cabinet are now in Brent's home, and they're still in mint condition. Dad's desk, solid and heavy, is mine, and my husband is distinctly uneager whenever I ask him to reposition it. My parents were on the "reduce, reuse, recycle" bandwagon long before it was fashionable, and their frugality sustained the heck out of their lifestyle. They never bought into consumerism—even when they could afford to in their later years. They didn't buy things to lift their moods or to feel better about themselves. By the time Dad retired, they could have stayed, thanks to God's blessings and to their talent for saving, in a luxury hotel on vacations, but they refused even to spring for Holiday Inn, preferring their old standby, Super 8. They were the antithesis of the "treat yourself, you deserve it" philosophy embraced by many people of my generation.

Giving was huge for my parents, but they didn't brag about it. In fact, they didn't talk about it much at all, but their actions made crystal clear the principle that God came first. After God, there were bills and food. Next was saving. After that, there wasn't anything left for extras—at least not in Westgate. At the one-year mark there, they had managed to set aside a few hundred dollars when my Grandma Schneller, uninsured, needed surgery. My parents used their savings to pay for it. Mom told me this in an off-hand remark when I was a teenager.

"Your parents took *all* your money?" I was shocked at my grand-parents' selfishness.

"No, Karen Ann," Mom answered. "Your father and I gave it to them."

"Why would you do that?"

"Because they needed it."

Thank goodness adolescence is temporary. Now, I can't imagine a scenario in which I wouldn't have given my last cent, or even one of my kidneys, to save my parents from poverty or sickness.

❧

St. Peter Lutheran Church was old-fashioned, even for the early 1960s. Men called each other by their first names except for my dad, who was always "Pastor." Women, or ladies, as they were labeled back then, addressed each other in person as Mrs. Whomever. In print, they were identified by their husbands' names.

When my mom died, I inherited her collection of church cookbooks. One was published by the Dorcas Society ladies at St. Peter in 1967 and sent to my mom in Liberty, Missouri, where we were then living. A handful of women used their own first names for recipe submissions, but the majority chose instead to style themselves as "Mrs. (insert husband's first name and their last name here)." The collection of recipes is a fascinating insight into a time that preceded Pinterest, Title IX, and, certainly for Westgate, the sexual revolution.

Mrs. Lorenz Reinking submitted a recipe for sour cream apple pie, which my mom judged "very good" along with Mrs. Carl Nauholz's six-layer surprise casserole. Based on Mom's "just fair" notes penciled in the cookbook margins, Mrs. Henry Reinking's Best Meatloaf and Mrs. Norman Fink's Delicious Oatmeal Pie must not have lived up to their names.

The cookbook is rife with puzzling and entertaining tidbits. There are, for instance, a surprising number of "Chinese" recipes in this German Lutheran collection, all containing ingredients no self-respecting Shanghai or Guangzhou cook would ever use. For instance, one woman's chow mein casserole is a concoction of ground beef, cream of mushroom soup, chicken noodle soup, rice, and soy sauce.[2] Eating this must have felt like a trip to the Forbidden City! Other oddities are Teen Bean Bake with Mom's accompanying note suggesting that it be served "with hamburgers—a teen favorite." I think this illustrates how innocent and uncomplicated teenagers, and adults, were then compared to now—or even compared to when I was that age. I would have scoffed loud and long if my mother had submitted anything that lame to a church cookbook. Mom graded the hamburger recipe "good," leaving me to wonder why on earth she needed a recipe for hamburgers. Another recipe in the spiral-bound compendium, One Dish Meal, calls for twenty-five cups of ham and feeds seventy-five people. I have no idea what Pie Plant is but, when combined with four cups of sugar and one 29¢ package of candy orange slices, it makes "delicious" jam.[3] More recipes than I care to dwell on include cream of chicken condensed soup, a product that my husband and I call "respiratory infection in a can" due to its unfortunate color and consistency. Anytime I cook with condensed anything, I want to drink copious amounts of Lush Slush, a recipe for which my contemporary fellow Lutheran, Mrs. Doug Mueller, has long been appreciated in our family. It's "intoxicatingly good."

My grandmothers didn't use recipes. They cooked with what they butchered, grew, and canned. My mom's generation was eager to use nifty kitchen appliances to whip up dishes made from convenient, processed ingredients. Mom was proud of her only kitchen gizmo, an electric knife, which she removed from its box only on Christmas, Easter, and Thanksgiving when she directed my dad to slice our turkey or ham. It was an even more useless appliance than the panini maker, electric rice steamer, and waffle iron I store in the recesses of my kitchen cabinets. Women my age and younger, while busy, have pampered lives compared to our predecessors and often manage to do half the work in twice as much time. Many of us don't cook as often as we know we should, but at least we have the self-awareness to feel guilty about it.

Although services at St. Peter were conducted in English, church records were kept in German. My baptism was recorded in German, and many older congregants spoke broken English or none at all. Dad made regular shut-in visits to one of the men who spoke only German.

Chris Thiessen took communion at home where his furniture consisted of chairs and tables formed from old orange and apple crates. His worn and stained German Bible always lay open on top of the crate that served as an end table. Mr. Thiessen liked to tell my dad that the problem with the world was that there wasn't enough bacon grease smeared in people's Bibles. I didn't understand what that meant when I was a child.

"It means don't be afraid to use your Bible and get it dirty," Dad told me. "It's not meant to be a decorative object."

When people commune at home, it generally means they are too old or frail to go to church. So, naturally, my dad didn't expect Mr. Thiessen to kneel to receive the sacrament. Every time, however, the octogenarian braced himself on a flimsy crate and sank to his knees in reverence. He took communion seriously—as did the entire congregation.

The current practice of "announcing for communion" (signaling one's desire to participate on any given Sunday) in most LCMS congregations entails filling out a card that can be found somewhere in the church pew and dropping it in the offering plate. But in Westgate in 1963, things were a tad more formal.

It was a long-standing practice at St. Peter that anyone planning to receive communion on the one Sunday a month it was offered had to announce their intent in person at the parsonage on the Friday or Saturday prior. My ten-year-old brother was assigned the role of greeter. He met people at the front door and showed them into Dad's study. If there was a backlog, Brent invited any waiting congregants to have a seat in one of the chairs on the large, enclosed front porch, and he engaged them in pleasantries while they anticipated their turn. Once in the study, a person would state their intent to commune and sometimes make a private confession. Knowing my dad, sports and gardening may also have been covered. Each session lasted about fifteen minutes. Brent enjoyed his role as doorkeeper, and it was something he missed when our family moved from Westgate.

As a newly minted pastor's wife, Mom was determined to excel at her role. One of her primary objectives was to produce ideal pastor's children. Brent bore the brunt of her efforts to showcase neat, clean, and perfectly behaved offspring who would be a credit to their father. Mom placed special emphasis on the neat and clean bit. No one in our family had much to wear, except for me, who had received, no joke, more than one hundred dresses at the baby shower held for my mom two weeks after my birth. Dad had one tired, threadbare suit; Mom had a few nice, but outmoded dresses; Brent had an outfit for church and a couple of changes of clothes for school. He was required to keep his attire stain-free, and our parents made him polish his shoes every Saturday evening.

Anyone who has a son knows how difficult it is for him to keep his clothing clean. It's an impossibility, really, if he is to have any fun during childhood. But whether due to a need for economy or to keep up appearances, or both, Mom drilled into Brent that his clothing must be pristine. This proved problematic for him at school one day when, playing tag at recess, a classmate accidentally grabbed his shirt and tore it. Panicked, Brent pushed the kid to the ground, sat on his chest, and punched him repeatedly. Mom was doubly upset. Brent's shirt required repair, and he had caused trouble at school—what would people think?

Upon arrival in Westgate, Mom's primary admonition to Brent was, "Remember, people are watching you." She modified this when I was older to, "Remember what people are thinking about your behavior, young lady." Consequently, Brent and I worry too much about what people think of us even now. We're both reserved and introverted, and we share a special understanding of each other and what makes us tick. When we lived in Michigan, one of Brent's high school friends "got his girlfriend pregnant" (she, ostensibly, had nothing to do with it). Mom told Brent *he* had better not do that. She also used this occasion to warn me that *I* had better not get pregnant. Because this was pre-internet 1972 and I was only eight years old, I wasn't even sure how that could happen, but I worried about it anyway.

As much as our mother cared about what people thought, our dad cared very little. Dad never lost his inner rebel, so maybe that's why he sent Brent to the store in Westgate to buy his unfiltered Camel cigarettes. (There was no law at the time preventing a ten-year-old from purchasing tobacco products.) Dad probably thought, "If people want to talk, let's give them something to talk about." Or, he knew how uptight my mom was about appearances, and he was trying to mitigate the baggage she was loading onto her son's young shoulders. Dad was sensitive to the expectations placed on Brent and me by our mom and by the members at any of the congregations where he served. For example, two things Brent was told ad nauseum were, "You look exactly like your father," and "You're going to be a pastor just like your dad!" Substitute the word "grandpa" for "dad," and that's what my son, who looks remarkably like my dad, has heard all his life. He dislikes it as much as I hated being told what a good pastor's wife I would make—something that literally made me ill.

When I graduated from high school, I was awarded a decent scholarship to attend my parents' alma mater, St. John's College, and I applied and was accepted there. I had no intention of going into church work or marrying anyone who was, but the school had a business program; and, like 99 percent of my friends, I was thinking of majoring in business, so why not go someplace where I had a scholarship? My parents weren't displeased with my decision, but, even though they didn't say so, I could tell they were surprised.

I do not exaggerate when I say that, once word got out that I was enrolled at a Lutheran college, every Sunday people came up to me at church and told me I was going to come home at Christmas with a pre-ministerial student. They teased me that I'd be married to a pastor in a few years. As the weeks went on, I became withdrawn and had trouble eating and sleeping. When I did eat, I threw up. I looked great in a pair of shorts and a tube top, but the unattractive dark circles under my eyes did nothing for me. I was thankful when my parents finally spoke up.

"Karen Ann, *what* is going on?" my mom demanded one night at dinner. "Your father and I are worried sick about you."

"I can't do it," I answered. "I can't go to St. John's. It's not the life I want."

"Have you been worried about this all summer?" Mom asked. "*Honestly*, Karen Ann, I was afraid you were dying!" (If you're wondering why it took so long for her to address her concerns, it's because she valued privacy as much as she did thrift and tidiness. And she trusted me to come clean when I was ready.)

My dad chimed in to say that he hoped they hadn't pressured me to make a choice that wasn't right for me.

"No, you guys didn't pressure me," I explained. "But you both love the place so much that when I got the scholarship, I thought it would make you happy."

"Frankly, we were shocked when you said you wanted to go there," Mom said.

"You aren't mad at me?"

They both assured me they were relieved, not mad.

"Can you imagine Karen being married to a pastor, Marvin?" Mom chortled. "It would be a disaster."

"I'll say," Dad responded, and they both had a good laugh at the thought of me making a mess of a hypothetical congregation and marriage.

My mom, who mellowed considerably over the years, knew more than anyone that I would despise the expectations placed on me if I married a pastor. She did a good job in her role, but she received her share of disapproval during my dad's ministry. I heard many criticisms over the years, *sotto voce* gossip among women in the church narthex who were either unaware or uncaring that I was standing close enough to hear them complain that my mom should be teaching Sunday school or doing more within the women's league. I hurt the most for my frugal mother when she and I both overheard one lady denouncing her for wearing a new store-bought dress to church. When I gave my dad an indignant earful at dinner that Sunday, he told Mom that he hoped she'd go out and buy another new dress that week.

Chapter Six

Disparate Housewives

Mom and me, Westgate, Iowa, 1965

On October 11, 1964, the *Des Moines Register* ran in its Sunday Home and Family section an article titled, "The Exacting and Rewarding World of the Minister's Wife." It's a revealing glimpse at how different the lives of these women were compared to pastors' wives of other generations. Interspersed with advertisements for 77¢ cotton bras and eight-dollar stretch panel girdles are anonymous quotes from half a dozen pastors' wives. One woman says having a job outside the home would undermine her husband as a leader. Another talks about how her introversion is an impediment to her role. A grateful mother states how glad she is that her children don't have to wear clothing from the church missionary barrel.[1] The article profiled two women in depth—one from an urban congregation and one from rural Iowa. Mrs. Dendy (Eleanor) Garrett, a Methodist from Des Moines, spoke about city ministry, and my mom represented the rural perspective.

Mrs. Dendy Garrett (her, or rather her husband's, full name repeated in the article to a comical degree) was probably ten years my mom's senior, but in her trendy Jackie Kennedy-inspired suits, she looked decades cooler. My mom, who at that time sewed all her clothing, epitomized "fashion-backward." Her crazy cat-eye glasses didn't help.

Mrs. Garrett studied journalism at Temple University in Philadelphia and participated in the 1963 March on Washington, where Martin Luther King Jr. delivered his "I Have a Dream" speech. She is quoted in the article regarding her role as a minister's wife, "Where else can a wife share her husband's work more completely?"[2]

My mom, as I've mentioned, was only allowed to attend college with the proviso that she become a teacher. While the future Mrs. Dendy Garrett worked toward an exciting career of her choosing, Mom was studying for something she didn't want to do, and she happily gave up teaching when Dad was ordained. In the article, she doesn't talk about sharing ministry but speaks about keeping "a calm, pleasant home setting." She eschews holding any church office because "this can harm the pastor."[3]

Photos show both women fulfilling their respective roles as helpers to their husbands. Mrs. Dendy Garrett meets with her group of ethnically diverse friends while my mom attends a typically homogeneous meeting of Lutheran women. Mrs. Garrett enjoys making an Indian corn and turkey feather Sunday school craft with two grumpy-looking children while Mom and my brother play Scrabble at the kitchen table[4], the overhead portrait of Jesus perfectly placed to deter cheating.

During my childhood, I regularly pulled out the *Register* article that my dad kept in his desk. I considered Mrs. Dendy Garrett my mom's rival, and I couldn't stand her. I wondered what the paper's readers made of these two women. Did they look at the city pastor's wife and think, "She has got it going on!"? Was my mom's traditional role met with scorn or respect?

Despite her conventional tendencies, I have always regarded my mom as something of a feminist. She and my dad certainly had an equal partnership. Before they married, Mom insisted on having money to do with as she pleased. Having had guilt heaped on her by her parents whenever she needed a pair of glasses or some school supplies made her loath to account to her husband for any purchases.

Mom derived satisfaction from her role as a pastor's wife, but she enjoyed it less as she aged. She was ready for my dad to retire so that she, too, could step down from the job. She regretted never having any deep friendships during my dad's ministry. Instructors at the seminary used to counsel that an effective pastor and his wife should never bond with anyone in the congregation. The instructors' view was that such friendships could breed contempt or jealousy. There is legitimacy in that view, but it's sad, nonetheless. Because it was de facto policy that she shouldn't get too close to anyone, Mom often came across as prickly, prissy, and reserved. She was every one of those things on occasion, but it's too bad she never felt free enough to let down her guard so people could experience her intelligence, dry wit, and generosity.

My dad would have been a good pastor, no matter what. He had the skills, gifts, and humility necessary for success. He would not, however, have been a great pastor without my mom. She didn't give him sermon ideas or advice on how to handle church business. My parents didn't discuss things of doctrinal heft at the dinner table. Rather, Mom was a confidante, and she knew how to keep her mouth shut. She never complained that Dad was away most nights for meetings or that we couldn't leave town on holidays because he had to preach. Unless we were on vacation, she never sat with her husband in church or took communion with him. She didn't blame Dad when our special family occasions took a back seat to others' family problems.

In my dad's retirement sermon, he talked about what my mom meant to him:

"Let me tell you something, folks. You cannot deal as a pastor with crises in people's lives if you have one of your own. You cannot bring peace to the parish if there is not peace in the parsonage. You cannot deal with the purposes of God if the purposes of your spouse run counter to it all. Admittedly, we, like all married couples, have our idiosyncrasies, which tend to be highlighted when we try to hang a curtain rod. But when it comes to the real issues, we have always read from the same page. What a blessing for the ministry, and what a gift from God."

When I watch the video of this sermon, I can't keep from crying because, as my dad preaches, the camera pans to my mom in the congregation. It's beautiful to see them there on DVD—together and alive, and palpably loving. My mom looks so proud and happy, and I realize it's her retirement day, too. She is lovely in a chic black suit from Macys—looking a good twenty years younger than she did in that feature article from 1964. Her job is complete, and she has made her sacrifices while finding joy and purpose along the way. She is a grown-up woman and a grown-up Christian. I will never be her equal in either respect.

Exactly one year after the *Des Moines Register* article ran, my dad received call papers from St. Stephen Lutheran Church in Liberty, Missouri, a town north of Kansas City. The call papers, which I found in my dad's files after he died, give practical details about the congregation, the church building, and the parsonage. Young congregation, good choir, willingness to try new things, folding chairs rather than pews in the sanctuary, new parsonage, good closet space. A line in the call agreement specifies that church services must be conducted in English. Under the "Financial" heading, $325 is offered as a base salary with an additional ten dollars per month for each child and five additional dollars per month for each year since ordination, making my dad's possible salary $355 per month. The church also provided $75 per month for a car allowance and paid all utilities. This was a fortune compared to what our family was living on in Westgate. A salary above the poverty line and a larger town where nosy people didn't inventory the contents of our grocery cart? It was a no-brainer. Dad accepted the call to Liberty.

He and my mom were excited about the move, but my brother was sad to leave Westgate. He loved the small town where, despite prying eyes, he had good friends and plenty of freedom.

On the day we drove out of Westgate, Dad sent Brent one last time to the store to buy a pack of cigarettes. Brent returned with the Camels and some canned meat, a good-bye gift from the proprietor. We hopped into our black 1963 Ford Galaxie 500—no seat belts or toddler booster seat, of course—and Dad steered south toward Kansas City.

Chapter Seven

On the Hill

St. Stephen Lutheran Church parsonage, Liberty, Missouri, c. 1968

After the fishbowl of Westgate, life at St. Stephen Lutheran
Church in Liberty was private, even isolated. The church,
and small parsonage directly across the gravel parking lot from it,
sat on one of the highest hills in town with an unobstructed view
of the Kansas City skyline. Except for that view to the south, we
were surrounded by woods. Not only did people not know, as they
had in Westgate, what groceries we consumed, but we could have

run a prostitution ring out of the parsonage, and no one would have had a clue.

I was almost two years old when we arrived in Liberty, and my memories of that first year are vague. By the time I turned three, I enjoyed roaming the nearly five-acre church property, feeling more adventurous than I really was. Throughout Brent's and my respective childhoods, Mom's cautionary mantra for us was, "Don't go near water. You'll drown." Although there wasn't any water on our hill, I extended Mom's admonition to include not climbing trees and not jumping off anything higher than a foot, supposing that any risk had no reward and that I'd end up critically injured or dead.

My dad installed a swing set for me in the backyard, but I preferred the old tire swing that hung from a large walnut tree at the edge of the woods. I spent what felt like hours on it—first straddling the rope on top of the tire, then lying on my stomach through the middle of the swing, my feet trailing patterns in the dirt.

"Why can't you play on your swing set, Karen Ann?" Mom asked every time I came inside with filthy shoes. "You make such a mess!"

When it rained, I walked over to the church to hang out with my dad in his office where I played with his limited batch of office supplies—pens, paper clips, and a stapler. Sometimes the church secretary let me help fold the freshly printed bulletins she had mimeographed for the coming Sunday. It's commonly said that of the five human senses, smell is the most evocative of memory. Anytime I encounter the pungent aroma of ink, I'm transported back to those hot summer mornings when I tried to get a perfect bulletin crease for Mrs. Magorian.

One day I was unusually restless, so I found a box of used crayons and attempted to sharpen them in the wall-mounted pencil sharpeners in each of the Sunday school classrooms. They all got stuck. A few days later, my dad mentioned at dinner, with a pointed look at me, that the janitor was unhappy because someone had messed up all the pencil sharpeners at church. I didn't repeat that stunt, no matter how bored I was.

Despite our almost ten-year age difference, my brother and I both looked forward to the annual church paper drive—two weeks each summer when a tractor trailer container was deposited on the parking lot so church members could rid themselves of their old newspapers and magazines and raise some money for the youth group. It was the perfect playground for me—a place to jump from the tall stacks of paper onto the soft piles below without fear of breaking a leg. I don't recall my parents ever cautioning me not to play in the container. My memory tells me the doors on the end were secured so I couldn't be trapped inside to die of heat exhaustion, but maybe that's wishful thinking that Mom and Dad weren't negligent. Brent was often inside with me, going through the contents in search of car magazines. His prize find one year was an STP oil sticker with the backing still on. He displayed it on his bedroom bulletin board for several years.

My parents were not pet people. Farm kids to the core, they regarded animals neither as companions nor as family members. Dad told me that when he was a child, one of their farm dogs spooked the horses that were hitched to the buggy. Grandpa Kuhlmann grabbed a shotgun and killed the dog on the spot. It sounds cruel *now*, but on a farm during the Depression a dead dog was preferable to a skittish, useless horse. Maybe my mom felt sorry for me, friendless up on the hill, because she readily let me make pets out of the plentiful box turtles around the property. I'd have four or five during any given summer. I was allowed to keep each one for a week or two before releasing it back outside. Most were small, with shells measuring four inches across, but several were more than twice that size. I was required to keep the turtles in a large box in the parsonage basement and let them out to roam the floor for a few hours of exercise each day, cleaning up after them. Mom permitted me to take lettuce scraps from the kitchen for them, but what really amazes me is that my pennywise mother bought Gaines-Burgers for me to give as treats. Her guilt over my lack of playmates must have been heavy, indeed, for her to spend money on dog hamburgers.

Snakes were abundant creatures near the parsonage, particularly blue racers. I haven't seen a blue racer since 1970 (thanks, in part, to my dad), but I saw plenty of them darting between rows of tomatoes and corn in Dad's garden in Liberty, and I can vouch that they live up to their name in both color and speed. Dad didn't enjoy harvesting vegetables and coming face-to-face with a snake, so he used his hoe to kill any he encountered. I remember standing next to him one summer evening in a row of beans while he talked to a church trustee, neither man bothered by the long, bloody blue racer hanging from the sharp point of the hoe. Dad loved statistics, and he kept track of his kills each year. His summer record, set in 1969, was forty-seven.

Liberty was oppressively hot in summer, especially inside the parsonage where we had no air-conditioning until the congregation installed a window unit in the kitchen. Even then, my mom suffered through canning season, sweat rolling down her cheeks as she stood over the stove, pressure cooker in use morning to late afternoon, days and weeks at a time. Beans, then pickles, and finally tomatoes, the hottest job of all—boiling water to remove the skins, and cooking the tomatoes in a large pot on the stove before sealing them in glass jars in the stovetop pressure cooker.

Storms were a temporary respite from the heat, but they were reliably severe in Clay County, Missouri. Tornado warnings were commonplace, and hail was frequently golf-ball-sized, and sometimes larger. I still love the unmistakable sound of hail raining down on a roof—rocks being hurled from the sky. My childlike enthusiasm is only slightly tempered now by adult thoughts of roof damage and insurance claims.

In Liberty, I was growing old enough to notice the storms going on in the world around me. An early reader, current affairs interested me even then. Apart from my dad's theology tomes, which were either dull or in Greek, Hebrew, or Latin, there wasn't much to read in the house except for the *Kansas City Times* and the *Kansas City Star*—the respective morning and afternoon newspapers. So, I read those, ignoring the comic strips except for the Crimestoppers feature in "Dick Tracy." Mom read "Mary Worth" for the pleasure of rolling her eyes at the old busybody. As for the news, I often didn't understand what I was reading, but we had stimulating discussions at dinner about world events, and I wanted to be conversant.

Tempestuous events marked 1968. Lyndon Johnson elected not to seek another presidential term. Martin Luther King Jr. was murdered in April, and riots erupted in dozens of cities, including Kansas City. Bobby Kennedy was assassinated in June. I tossed gravel in the parking lot after choir practice as Mom and several other women wept over another slain Kennedy. The U.S. was entrenched in Vietnam, and Mom worried about Brent. A few years later in Michigan, the war still raging and Brent possessing a low draft number, Mom noted the short distance to the Canadian border. My dad, not a fan of that war but a proponent of duty, was not on board with her train of thought. She may have made the statement offhandedly in a moment of anxiety, but a mother's heart can take her brain places that a father doesn't always comprehend. Brent wasn't drafted—he was headed to college and would have had a deferment. Furthermore, the draft ended during his senior year of high school. Half a century later, as a mother whose son will soon register for Selective Service, I understand why my mother, however briefly, considered defying the law to keep her child safe.

The following year, 1969, still saw the country divided by the war, but the first moon landing in July finally gave everyone a reason to celebrate. Taking a break from the continual TV coverage of mankind's most incredible technological achievement to date, my dad and I walked outside to gaze up at the moon. Even though I could read and knew more about world affairs than the average five-year-old, I was ignorant of the scale of the universe. The moon looked no farther away to me than the buildings in downtown Kansas City. I wondered aloud why I couldn't see the landing module from our spot on the church parking lot. Dad explained how far away Neil Armstrong and Buzz Aldrin were.

"That could be you up there someday," Dad said. "If that's what you want."

The thought of being in space terrified me, but my dad's belief that I could do something like that if I so desired made me happy in a quiet, confident way. He was the great encourager of my life.

❦

My parents, Mom especially, were all about routine. That makes sense given that Dad's life, and our lives, by extension, was ordered around evening meetings, hospital calls, office hours, and fitting in time to prepare at least one sermon per week—more during Advent and Lent and extras for any weddings or funerals.

One routine my parents cherished was cocktail time every afternoon before Mom made dinner. Dad mixed two Manhattans, each with two shots bourbon, one shot vermouth, and a maraschino cherry, and he and Mom settled into the orange-upholstered swivel chairs in the living room to discuss their respective days. I made sure to hang around listening to their tedious adult conversation because when Dad finished his drink, I was allowed to eat the alcohol-laden cherry. Sometimes he let me have a small sip of his Manhattan. I loved the taste of whiskey when I was a child but can't stand the stuff as an adult. It sounds ludicrous to give a youngster a taste of a potent drink, but children in German families histor-ically have been allowed this privilege. I was allotted a tiny glass of wine at Sunday dinner, and Dad, every time after mowing the lawn, poured a splash of his beer into the pink plastic cup from which I had gulped my Kool-Aid. My dad treasured his calling and the hard work it involved, and he loved the physical labor of mowing or working in his garden. I think he never felt more alive than on those hot summer evenings, covered in sweat and grass clippings and drinking a cold Budweiser. I believe that these were real moments of prayer and thanksgiving for him when he, in his words, drank a cold one "to the glory of God."

Mom didn't allow the TV to be on during the day, except for Saturday morning cartoons. That was fine by Brent and me because watching television at the parsonage in Liberty was not relaxing. To save the living room furniture from wear, Mom insisted that the TV be placed in the kitchen. So, we sat around the chrome and black table, chairs adjusted to face the black-and-white set, trying our best to get comfortable for an hour or two.

Our evening viewing was not democratic—we watched what Mom wanted to watch. This provided me with an excellent education about both historical and contemporary cultures. For example, I learned that ranchers in the late 1800s were unusually attractive and that men like Heath Barkley and Little Joe Cartwright could work their enormous spreads all day, and their clothing would still be pristine when they each came home to a nice dinner made by a domestic servant. I also discovered that handsome ranchers should never fall in love because their sweethearts would, without exception, be killed a few days before the wedding. TV shows that represented a more modern perspective also taught me important life truths. *Mary Tyler Moore*, *That Girl*, and *Petticoat Junction* established that single women have the best clothing and the most fun, while shows like *Medical Center* proved to be the WebMD of their day. That headache, rash, cough, or weird tingling sensation? That's right—it's cancer.

⁂

Shortly after we moved to Liberty, my parents purchased a used Apache fold-out camper. It was, with its two plywood bed frames and thin mattresses, to today's camper trailers what the Wright brothers' plane was to an F-16 fighter jet. But it was cheap and clean and would take us places. Dad and Mom, having grown up in households where nobody wanted to see the next state over, let alone the world, were adamant that their kids not be limited. We began alternating summer trips—one year to relatives and the next camping somewhere. Our first camping excursion, when I was two years old, was to Table Rock Lake in southern Missouri, where I proved to be an embarrassing travel companion. I can still feel the Silver Dollar City stagecoach driver's ire as he kicked us off his rig after I, riding shotgun with my dad, threw up all over myself, the bench seat, and some of the people inside the coach. The ridged scar on the back of my head reminds me of how I ignored my parents' warning to stop rocking side-to-side in my lawn chair at our rocky campsite, tipped over, and sliced my scalp. My bawling woke the entire campground. Mom and Dad were embarrassed but undeterred. One summer, we traveled to Colorado Springs, and the July before I started kindergarten we journeyed to South Dakota to see the Badlands, Mount Rushmore, and Flintstone Village. The

Barney Rubble car ride was the best part of the trip for me—until we visited my mom's college roommate on our way back to Missouri.

Dee had married a rodeo man, and they had five children, all between Brent and me in age. They were the most unusual people I had ever encountered. Their imposing black stallion, Dynamite, and beautiful, snow-white Daisy were the most impressive of their dozen or so show horses. Dee's three daughters had an entire out-building in which to store their rodeo costumes, and they took turns dressing me up in their finery. My favorite outfit was the gypsy costume with its veils and gold spangles. The girls begged my mom to allow me to ride a horse, but she refused, having been thrown from one as a child. One evening, the family staged their rodeo act for us—parading with flags and exhibiting trick riding and barrel racing.

A couple of days before we left for home, as I was conspiring with Dee's six-year-old son, Jeffrey, to run away with him and hide in the barn so that I could stay and be part of the rodeo gang, our two families toured nearby Gavins Point Dam on the Missouri River. The day was a scorcher, and several of us kids, ignoring our mothers' warnings about germs, shared a bottle of ice-cold Pepsi. The next morning, Dee and Mom hurried to empty the bowls of vomit we were producing at a prodigious rate. Too weak to escape my boring life and predictable parents, I abandoned my plan to flee and returned with them to Liberty where I would start school following Labor Day.

Chapter Eight

Learning Curve

The sign on the train says, "Not
responsible for accidents," 1969.
(I was, in fact, responsible for
numerous childhood accidents.)

Bored with roaming the church property by myself and tired
of begging my family to play Monopoly, I was ecstatic to be
starting school. With no neighbors, I only interacted with kids
my age one hour a week during Sunday school, and I longed for
company other than my parents and teenage brother.

On my first day of kindergarten, Dad waited with me for the
school bus at the end of the long driveway that curved down the

hill to the street below. Liberty's kindergarten buses featured animals rather than numerals, and I rode the Squirrel Bus, which my dad found hilarious. There was a black silhouette of a rodent with a long, bushy tail where a bus number would ordinarily be. That noon, upon arrival back at the parsonage, I proudly informed my parents that I was the only child who wasn't crying that morning and the only one who hadn't needed to be pried from their mother's or father's arms. I couldn't understand why my fellow kindergartners were upset. Didn't they know how much fun this was?

Mrs. Travis was my teacher, and I adored her. She was kind and patient, and she told vivid stories about the places where she and her husband planned to travel when he retired—especially England.

"Mrs. Travis is going to England next summer!" I told my mom over a lunch of sardine sandwiches the day my teacher had first talked about her vacation plans.

"She must have said Europe," Mom corrected. "Not England." She had more of an interest in traveling to the Continent than to Britain, so she assumed other people did, too.

"She didn't say that," I replied. "She said England!"

I was right about the destination—but I didn't expect Mrs. Travis to retire in the middle of the school year due to health problems. She seemed like a kindred soul, and I was sad to see her go. She was replaced by Mrs. Craft, the school principal. Where Mrs. Travis had been enthusiastic, Mrs. Craft was spiritless. Mrs. Travis had been warm and friendly, whereas Mrs. Craft was cool and all business. I wished with all my heart that *she* were the one with health problems.

My report card, up until January when Mrs. Craft took over, had been a sea of O's for "outstanding." But Mrs. Craft brooked no imperfection. She found my printing untidy, my lines on connect-the-dot worksheets too squiggly, and my aesthetic ability non-existent.

"You'll never be an artist," she told me as she assessed the water-color mess on my easel one day during art. She turned to lavish praise on the neighboring student who had, unlike me, painted something recognizable. Mrs. Craft was right—I had zero talent for drawing or painting. I even had trouble staying within the lines in my coloring books. But her criticism was discouraging, and I've avoided, except for Pictionary, any attempts at visual art ever since.

The best thing about kindergarten was that I finally had a friend. Marta was keen on being pals from the first day of school, and we were seatmates at one of the classroom tables. The social highlight of my year, of my life to that point, really, was Marta's sixth birthday party to which I was the only kid from class invited. I had never been to, or had, a birthday party.

I was bouncing off the parsonage walls by the time Marta and her dad came to pick me up for her evening party. She was excited, too—we both were grateful to have found a companion at school. Her dad wore a black leather jacket and promised my parents he would take good care of me and have me home in a couple of hours. When we arrived at Marta's house, I was ushered inside to meet grandparents, aunts, uncles, and cousins. Remember how I said that my Grandma Kuhlmann shook hands when greeting her own grandchildren? This gregarious Italian family treated me like the guest of honor—hugging me, pinching my cheeks, and kissing me. They were a boisterous group, and they made sure my plate was never empty. I shared more affection with them in those three hours than I had with my own extended family in a lifetime. It was an exhilarating day in my young life, and I arrived back at the parsonage on a high, wishing my family were more like Marta's.

"The cake had purple frosting, Mom!" I exulted. "And the inside was red!" My mom always appreciated a good food anecdote.

Dad was happy that I'd had a great time. He, probably more than Mom, saw how much I craved friendship. Thereafter, my parents made sure that we regularly invited Marta to the parsonage or to my favorite place on earth, Penguin Park (named for its twenty-five-foot-tall penguin edifice) in Kansas City.

At the end of the school year, our class walked the quarter mile to downtown Liberty to visit the Jesse James Bank Museum—the site of the first daylight bank robbery in the United States. I came away from the tour not knowing whether I was supposed to find the James Gang reprehensible or likable. After thirty minutes at the bank museum, we trudged over to the historic Liberty Jail where Joseph Smith, the founder of Mormonism, had been incarcerated in 1838. This had to be the most tedious, least fun kindergarten field trip ever and possibly why, to this day, I don't enjoy visiting museums.

The following September, I began first grade at Lewis and Clark Elementary School. I had the same bus stop, but this year Dad drove me down the hill each morning and was there in the afternoon when I disembarked the bus. He and Mom were keeping a closer eye on me when I played outside, too. A few months earlier, in the middle of the night, a man rang the parsonage doorbell. My dad, dressed in his pajamas, answered the door. The stranger said he'd been hiding in the woods near the house, watching our family for several days. He knew our routines, guessed correctly that we didn't have a dog, and probably figured my dad, being a pastor, was an easy mark. The man demanded our car and any cash on hand. Dad told the man to wait outside while he retrieved the car keys and rounded up some money. Dad assumed the phone line had been cut and was prepared to get his shotgun to defend his family, if necessary. However, the phone had a dial tone, so he called the police and then managed to stall the trespasser until Liberty's finest stormed up the hill. They stopped at the edge of the parsonage lawn, scrambled out of the cars with weapons drawn, and pushed the man up against the house's brick exterior before cuffing him. Our night visitor was wanted in seven states for a laundry list of crimes including armed robbery and burglary. We had dodged the proverbial bullet, and he had dodged a literal gunshot. Many people assume pastors are meek and pacifistic. Not my dad. He wouldn't have hesitated to put a shell in the guy if he had made a move to hurt any of us.

The next morning, I was angry I'd slept through the most exciting thing that had ever happened to our family—or possibly to anyone else I knew.

"Why didn't you wake me up?" I whined.

"It was for the best that you were sleeping," my mom answered. "I'm glad the noise didn't wake you."

I thought this was unfair. Now I realize Mom was probably playing all kinds of scenarios in her mind involving her six-year-old daughter traipsing through the woods, unaware a man was hiding and watching. Mom could be overbearing with her cautions and warnings, but she treasured her children. The thought of anything happening to Brent or me made her ill. She was extra vigilant after this incident, ironically curtailing my freedom after the threat had been neutralized. Now that I'm a mother, I don't fault her. In fact, I admire her restraint. I would have demanded that whatever rudimentary home security system existing in 1970 be installed at the parsonage, and I would have scrapped the no daytime TV rule, instead encouraging a gluttony of viewing so there would be no temptation to play outside in the woods.

In addition to less outdoor fun at home, school wasn't as enjoyable, either. I never saw Marta—she was in a different first grade group, and our paths didn't cross. So, I was a loner in class, at lunch, on the playground, and on the bus. After the first day, I sat on the bus waiting to leave the school parking lot when two smirking sixth grade boys in front of me turned around and told me I was on the wrong bus. I felt an instant of panic, but I calmly walked up the aisle to the driver and asked if this was bus number six. She assured me it was. I walked back to my seat and sassed to the boys that maybe *they* were on the wrong bus. When I recounted the incident to my parents, I could tell they were proud of how I had handled the situation. As an adult, I sometimes wonder where that ballsy little girl went. I miss her.

My teacher, Mrs. Morton, played favorites, and hers were the girls who dressed impeccably and whose hair was perfectly cut and styled. My mom's home-sewn creations, however expertly constructed, didn't impress her.

"Tell your mother to stop making so many blouses with short sleeves," she told me one morning. "It's too cold outside for those." And, "Why do you only have one pair of shoes? Most people have at least two."

Mrs. Morton clearly loved Patty Morris, the most popular girl in first grade. Patty was pretty, and regularly had a new outfit to add to her sizeable inventory of skirts and dresses. And in the ultra-Baptist town of Liberty, she went to the same Baptist church as Mrs. Morton.

Another advantage Patty had over me was a decent haircut. My naturally curly hair was getting long and unruly, and Mom was wearying of all the tangles, so she said we had to shorten it. To save money, Dad cut all our hair. He must not have been paying attention when, at the seminary, a fellow classmate and future Air Force chaplain (and father of NFL quarterback Danny Weurffel) barbered for extra cash. Dad knew one style—short. Following every hair trim, I shut myself in my bedroom to cry. I looked like a boy! I wanted long, straight hair like Patty had—she could wear ribbons and barrettes and look cute. I did what I could to look girly, at least at home. My mom, however, wasn't about to buy me any unnecessary accessories, so I found a way to acquire them.

If the church was locked when floral deliveries were made for funerals, the delivery man left the arrangements by the entry door. I didn't think anyone would miss a ribbon or two, so I made sure no one was watching and grabbed any pink or red ones. I fastened them to my hair with the floral wire, not bothering to remove the green wooden sticks that had anchored the ribbons to the plants or flowers. I thought I looked darling with the preposterous bows in my hair, so much that the "Beloved Father" and "Rest Peacefully" messages didn't bother me one bit.

First grade girls at Lewis and Clark could be junior cheerleaders. There were no tryouts—any girl could participate if her parents purchased the mandatory gold and green school sweatshirt and matching pom-poms. I wanted so badly to be a junior cheerleader, but I didn't bother asking my parents. There was no way Donna Kuhlmann was going to spend money on a school sweatshirt, and I didn't want to feel the disappointment of being told "no." So, I sat on a bench in the school gym with a couple of other girls and watched Patty and her crew run through cheers for the sixth grade boys while they played basketball during PE.

The class Christmas party was touted as the best day of the school year, and I almost missed it. A few days prior, I had made the mistake of informing my fellow classmate Janie that Santa Claus was not real. My parents never bothered doing the Santa thing for me. They both had grown up with the German version of Santa, and they had encouraged Brent to believe in him. When they finally told my brother that Santa wasn't real, he asked if Jesus was fake, too. So, when Janie was going on and on about Santa coming to her house on Christmas, I told her the truth. I didn't taunt or tease her—I merely relayed the information as I would have if she had given the wrong answer to a math problem. Janie started sobbing, and her friends ratted me out to Mrs. Morton, who, after threatening to ban me from the class party, made me stand in the corner for what seemed an eternity.

She relented, and I did get to participate in the party, but now I had a bad reputation with the room mothers, one of whom was Janie's mom. The party was a dud—we each had a dry, store-bought cookie and a cup of fruit punch. The best part was the drawing of numbers for the gift exchange. Boys drew for boy gifts and girls for girl gifts. I drew number one for the girls, and I had to walk past perfect Patty to get to the Christmas tree.

"Good things come in *small* packages," she said as I selected the largest girl present under the tree. My comeback game has always been lousy, so I ignored her on the way back to my chair. When it was her turn, Patty picked the smallest box, which contained a "real diamond necklace." Mrs. Morton and the other girls admired it as they sipped more punch and waited for the bell to ring for Christmas break. I didn't care about the necklace. I was thrilled with my prize—a board game involving circus wagons, caged animals, and banana game pieces. I hoped I could coerce my family into playing it with me.

Two months later, my dad received a call to serve as pastor of a congregation in Flint, Michigan. It was larger than St. Stephen and had a K-8 school. The challenge appealed to my dad, Brent didn't mind moving, and I was up for something new. The church and parsonage were situated in an actual neighborhood, and I hoped to make a friend or two. Mom, however, didn't want to leave Liberty. She watched from the living room window as Dad returned from the Sunday afternoon church voters' meeting where he had informed the group that he was taking the call to Flint. Mom was praying he would walk in the door and announce that he had changed his mind and decided we should stay. But

God was leading him to make the move, and we prepared for our departure.

Mrs. Morton was nice to me on my final day at Lewis and Clark. I was allowed to act as class library helper—my favorite job. I was finally able to convince someone to check out the orange book with the bad pen and ink illustrations that was always overlooked in the two-shelf classroom bookcase. Books were, by this time, my favorite companions. My mom permitted me to order two books whenever the Scholastic Book Catalog was handed out at school, and I was accruing a small library in my bedroom, augmented by any books received as Christmas or birthday gifts. I envied Mrs. Morton for her teacher's edition of short stories, poems, and songs. The book, spiral-bound and open on the corner of her desk, still seizes my imagination when I remember the red, blue, and yellow drawings and green type. I'd love to leaf through it now, running my hands over the thick, waxy pages and stopping to read "The Owl and the Pussycat" or the lyrics to "This Land is Your Land." I have coveted few things in life, but that magical book is one of them.

Chapter Nine

I Don't Want to Have the Prayer

Praying my brother doesn't eat
all my birthday cake, 1966

I had no regrets about leaving Mrs. Morton behind, but I was
going to miss my Sunday school teacher. Mary Smith looked
like my mom—a slim brunette with short curly hair—but was
more patient. She drove a white VW Beetle, and when I think of
prayer, I think of her.

I'm not good at prayer. My dad was gifted at prayer, but that doesn't mean he sat around all day with his hands folded and head bowed. In fact, Dad believed God endowed us with the requisite common sense to make some decisions without Divine consultation.

"If I see that my car is dirty, I'm not going to pray about it—I'm going to grab a bucket of water and wash the car." This was his way of explaining to his young daughter that answers to difficulties often are obvious, and we shouldn't have to ask God to provide a solution. We just need to get the job done. "Pray, but bring your checkbook," was his admonition whenever a congregation sought his advice, and the Lord's help, with fundraising.

When my husband and I went furniture shopping a few weeks after our wedding, we found a couch and coffee table that met our needs in a hunter green and heavy, brown, claw-footed sort of way. Jim was hesitant about pulling the trigger, though.

"Maybe we should go home and pray about it," he said to my astonishment. Jim had yet to become a Lutheran, and his Baptist upbringing was rearing its head.

"Pray about a *coffee table?*" We needed some decent furnishings. I was tired of his card table, cinder blocks, and the 1965 gold vinyl ottoman that his parents handed down to him when he rented his first apartment. "No, we do *not* need to pray about it."

Some people are gifted at prayer just as others are gifted at hospitality or teaching. Although prayer isn't my strong suit, I wish it were. Being a pastor's kid, however, seems to give people the impression of a genetic pre-disposition toward intercessory excellence. Since childhood, I've been called upon to pray on numerous occasions. At St. Mark Lutheran School in Flint, if no other child volunteered to lead the class in prayer, I was selected to do the honors. At Holy Trinity Lutheran in Grandview, Missouri, I was routinely asked to have a prayer at senior high youth events. My "favorite" request was made by two of my public high school English teachers right before a National Honor Society banquet. They asked me to hang back on the school bus that had transported our group to Stephenson's Apple Farm restaurant in Kansas City. I thought I was in trouble, although I couldn't imagine why.

"Karen," Mrs. Dunnington began, "we thought you would like to have the prayer before our meal."

"No, thank you," I politely responded.

"We really think you're the one to do it," Mrs. Willard chimed in.

"No."

I was a completely caught-off-guard seventeen-year-old. I did not want to have the prayer and had neither the desire nor the maturity to explain why, so I waited silently as they stared at me until they gave up and let me exit the bus. When our group sat down to dinner, Mrs. Dunnington announced we would have a moment of silence. When I arrived home later that evening, I made the mistake of telling my dad, within earshot of my mom, what had transpired.

"You didn't have the prayer, Karen Ann—why *not*?" She was appalled. "You're perfectly capable of praying. Do you want people to think you don't care about God?"

Yep. That had been my aim exactly. To make people think I didn't care about God.

"Marvin, she should have had the prayer!"

My dad impatiently set aside the Kansas City Royals box score he had been studying.

"Why?" he asked. "It was unfair of them to put her on the spot like that." He paused to take a sip of his evening coffee. "They were uncomfortable and didn't want to do it, but they didn't mind making your daughter uncomfortable."

To this day, I appreciate those friends with whom I lunch who don't go in for praying aloud in restaurants. They never give me the "you pray" look. I'm not embarrassed to pray publicly, and I can string together a prayer that sounds decent—not that eloquence is what matters. But I still recoil from any expectation that *I'm* the one to pray because of some talent that supposedly comes from being pastor-adjacent.

Two prayers have been a constant in my life. "Now I Lay Me Down to Sleep" has been a bedtime practice since my parents taught it to me before I could even talk. Some parents now use an amended version of this prayer—one that omits the words, "If I should die before I wake," presumably so their young children don't worry about dying in their sleep. It never occurred to me when I was a child that I might die before morning. When our son was born, Jim and I received as a gift a stuffed elephant that, when wound, recited the arguably more palatable version of the prayer which, instead of death before waking, speaks of angels watching through the night and waking the child with the morning light. Nice words, but the disembodied voice coming from our elephant was weirdly full of saliva and malice—scarier than any reference to death.

The other prayer that runs through my brain before trying to fall asleep is the second verse of the hymn "Now the Light Has Gone

Away," which is usually sung within the LCMS at evening church services during Advent or Lent. Penned by Frances R. Havergal in 1869, it is set to the German tune "Müde bin Ich"—literally, "I am tired." Mrs. Smith taught our Sunday school class to pray the second verse of this hymn as a bedtime prayer:

———◆◆———

"Jesus, Savior, wash away
All that has been wrong today;
Help me every day to be
Good and gentle, more like Thee."

———◆◆———

This prayer has influenced me nearly every day of my life. I'm thankful I had the opportunity to say that to Mrs. Smith when she filed through the line in front of my dad's coffin at his visitation. We don't always get to thank the people who have made a difference in our lives because we don't recognize the importance of a moment of instruction, or grace, or mercy until we're old enough, or ready enough, to grasp its significance. The prayers of childhood are the most meaningful of my adult life. I've spent plenty of time telling myself that I need to be a better Christian, a better wife, a better mother, and, yes, better at prayer. I *am* good at praying from a position of fear or worry—but not so good at praying from a place of trust. In their simplicity, the nighttime prayers taught to me at an age when faith felt as it ought to feel—easy and uncomplicated—have become more of a message from God to me rather than something I'm saying to Him.

"Stop dissecting your life trying to find where you think you fall short, and give yourself a break," He tells me. "Go to sleep and get some rest—because that's what I'm all about."

And all God's people—especially *this* gal who has, daily and without fail, received every good thing from His bountiful and loving hand—say, "Amen."

Chapter Ten

Finding My Bearings

Brent, Mom, me, and Dad at St. Mark, Flint,
Michigan, installation reception, 1971

It used to be that, in the Missouri Synod, pastors did not visit congregations prior to accepting or declining a Divine Call. Demonstrating what, exactly? That to make an informed decision about vocation, housing, and schooling shows a lack of faith? Whatever the reason, when my dad turned our Ford LTD onto Daly Boulevard in Flint, Michigan, the site of our new, and heretofore unseen, congregation and parsonage, part of my mom died. She may have been expecting her surroundings to reflect the street's stately name—"boulevard" sounds like it should feature trees and fountains and, at the very least, a paved surface. Not this one. You know those photos of mining towns from the Gold Rush era, the ones with sloppy, muddy streets and dirty puddles everywhere? That's what Daly Boulevard resembled when we arrived that dismal March afternoon.

The aluminum-sided parsonage looked nice, although the tri-level's exterior had a peculiar color scheme. One half of the house was pale pink while the other half was failing in its attempt to be yellow. There was no landscaping to clash with the hues, so that was a plus. Dad parked the car and trailing Apache camper on the asphalt driveway. It strikes me that until I was eighteen years old and my parents purchased a home, they never referred to where we lived as "our house." Neither did the people at any of the congregations my dad served. It was always "the parsonage." And of course, it was always next to the church. People often dropped by during the day, during dinner, or after 9:00 p.m. when Mom was finally ready to relax. Instead, she felt compelled to brew coffee and provide snacks.

At none of the parsonages during my dad's ministry did we feel like we had any privacy. When, in my teenage years, we lived at the parsonage at Holy Trinity Lutheran Church in Grandview, Missouri (where the distance from the church could be bridged with a decent tape measure), Henry Holz, a sociable Texan and church member, dropped by one summer morning to see the pastor. My mom, who then had a job as a dental assistant and wasn't home at the time, sternly informed me at dinner that evening that the poor man had stood ringing the parsonage doorbell for five minutes. I hadn't heard it over the REO Speedwagon album I'd been blasting on my stereo. Mr. Holz had heard the racket and, after tiring of leaning on the buzzer, stormed over to the church and demanded of the secretary, "What the HELL is going on at the parsonage?"

My dad thought this was funny. Mom was embarrassed and worried about what people would think if the story circulated, but her irritation at our lack of privacy won out. Neither of my parents even *hinted* that I should turn down the music.

At least in Flint, a half-acre plot separated the parsonage from the church. In our seven years there, Dad, Brent, and I usually cut across the grass on our way to meetings or worship services. In fair, dry weather, Mom walked the dirt road. She drove to church the other fifty Sundays of the year.

Flint has, in recent years, become famous for its decline. In 1970, the year before we moved there, Flint had almost 200,000 residents. Its 2017 population was less than 100,000.[1] In 2015, toxic levels of lead were found in the city's drinking water. That crisis, along with fallout associated with the city's high levels of poverty and crime, is soberly and expertly recorded in the Netflix documentary *Flint Town*.

General Motors was the only show in town when we lived in Flint. The automobile industry was paramount, and kids aspired to follow in their parents' footsteps, eschewing college to work on the line. My dad used to ponder the dearth of economic diversity in Flint, correctly guessing that the town would be in trouble if GM closed up shop. Today, whenever I meet someone who has Michigan ties, and I try to create five minutes' worth of camaraderie, I mention I lived for a while in that state. Their faces generally fall when I tell them I lived in Flint. Although I wouldn't want to live there now, I loved the city, and most things about our congregation, during our time in Flint.

✹

The movers arrived in Flint with our possessions three days after we did. Following a few nights at a Howard Johnson's, we were able to unpack our clothing and furniture before Dad was installed as pastor at St. Mark. He and my brother were given the customary white carnation boutonnieres by the altar guild while Mom and I each received a pink-and-white corsage. I don't think that's done much anymore for installations or ordinations, which is too bad—I always felt grown up with a carnation pinned to my dress. Old photos of that day reveal me in all my dweeby glory. My hair, courtesy of my dad, was freshly shorn, and I wore a homemade green double-knit jumper, white Peter Pan collar blouse, white socks, and scruffy shoes. At the dinner following the service, my Lutheran school classmates, who sang for the event and whom I would meet the following Tuesday when I started school, sized me up like I was fresh meat in a prison yard.

✹

A kid named Gerry showed up early Monday morning at the parsonage. His family attended St. Mark, and his mom had instructed him to walk with Brent to Kearsley High School, located at the east end of Daly Boulevard. She had also given Gerry orders to be nice to the new pastor's son. Gerry had unkempt hair and wore scruffy bell-bottom jeans, reminding me of Shaggy from *Scooby-Doo.* He didn't look any different from most Flint teenagers in 1971, but he dressed far less conservatively than had the kids in Liberty. He and Brent ambled down the street to school and into a lifelong friendship.

The following day, after Gerry again stopped for Brent, another visitor arrived. My dad opened the front door to reveal the old lady (she was probably fifty) who lived in the corner house with its overgrown yard. She told Dad she had spied Gerry at the parsonage two days in a row to "walk your boy" to school. I stood next to my dad as the woman gave a report of Gerry and teenage debauchery. She warned that Brent would soon fall prey to all manner of vice. Whoa—this was exciting and dangerous stuff! As our neighbor continued to spin her tales of adolescent bacchanalia, I noticed my dad seemed unconcerned about Brent's friendship with Gerry. Instead, he appeared irritated that this woman was all up in our business. He thanked her for stopping by and moved to shut the door.

"Don't say I didn't warn you!" she hissed over her shoulder as she turned to leave.

It was a foggy Michigan morning, and I, under the influence of my love for eerie books, wished her departure had included a swirling black cape and an ominous soundtrack. Unfortunately, there was no sinister music, and she wore a baby-blue housecoat with matching dingy scuffs. But the hissing, the mist, and her dramatic warning were so exciting I could hardly stand it. Life here was going to be fascinating!

Just as my dad was ready to walk me to school, the doorbell rang again, and I answered it, hoping it was the nosy neighbor. A different woman, this one holding two over-stuffed black garbage bags, introduced herself as Mrs. Mann and said she needed to speak with my mother about me. I yelled to my mom to come to the door and waited there, wanting to discover what the conversation had to do with me and dying to know what was in the trash sacks. Mom greeted Mrs. Mann, who handed over the bags, explaining they contained clothing that her daughter, Kimmie, had outgrown. Mrs. Mann told me I would meet Kimmie at school as she was in the third grade, two years ahead of me. Kimmie's brother, Kurt, was in my grade and in the high reading group with the best grades in class.

"Don't worry if you aren't able to keep up with him," she advised me.

I kept my sassy thoughts to myself and smiled meekly at Mrs. Mann, too preoccupied with the contents of the plastic bags to be offended by her inference that I was not as clever as her son. I wondered if she had noticed me in my plain jumper at the installation service and had taken pity on me. My mom was a talented seamstress, but serviceability, rather than style, was her objective when making my clothes. While Mrs. Mann filled my mom in on Kimmie's competitive figure skating exploits, I stood there fantasizing about sequins, rhinestones, and feathers—all a world away from the cottons and double-knits that made up my wardrobe. Other than when I was an infant, and except for socks, underwear, and winter coats, I had never had a store-bought piece of clothing. I could not wait to get my hands on those trash bags!

"Anyway," Mrs. Mann concluded, bringing my attention back to the conversation, "I thought you might need them."

I thought it was strange that my mom didn't seem overwhelmed with gratitude at this windfall. She politely thanked our benefactor for thinking of us, called to my dad that it was time to walk me to school, and shot me her "we'll talk about this later" look.

Dad and I sauntered across the empty lot, and he made sure I was settled in my classroom. Before heading to his office, he introduced me to my teacher, Mrs. Pohlmann. She, like my Sunday school teacher in Liberty, looked remarkably like my mom, although to a six-year-old everyone older than thirty looks the same. Mrs. Pohlmann welcomed me to class and told me she had a present for me. She reached under her desk and lugged out a large box with flaps for lids.

"It's a beer box!" she exclaimed.

I didn't know what to say, so I stood there waiting for my teacher to elaborate. Why was she giving me a beer box? Was there beer in it? I didn't think my parents would allow me to have an entire box of beer.

"It's for you to store your textbooks and school supplies," Mrs. Pohlmann explained as I caught the looks that passed among my eighteen first and second grade classmates—the looks that said, "check out this loser."

Mrs. Pohlmann confessed she had forgotten to inform my parents that they needed to send something with me every day for the mid-morning snack break. But no problem—she had extras in her desk from which I could choose this one time. She proffered two items—a Golden Delicious apple and a mini box of Sun-Maid raisins. Unaware I was making a freakishly aberrant selection, I reached for the raisins. I heard muffled laughter and a sarcastic, "She *would.*"

I took the snack, and Mrs. Pohlmann carried the beer box to my desk. I focused on my desktop to avoid making eye contact with the hostiles. The beer boxes, I learned, were used in lieu of lockers and could be decorated as desired with paint or wallpaper. This being 1971, most kids had painted their boxes orange, gold, or green while others had covered theirs in flocked wallpaper. My beer box was solid white, like every wall in every parsonage we had ever lived.

I sat quietly, listening to the morning devotion while the boys stared at me and the girls appraised me, giggling and whispering to each other behind their hands. I made for good fodder. A socially inept child, I didn't know how to interact with kids my age. (On the other hand, I killed it with the over-forty crowd.) I dressed more modestly than the other girls, and my desire for friendship was palpable. Those former traits probably didn't mean much, but the latter is the proverbial blood in the water of the shark pool of childhood. My classmates were ready to feed, and I was the jumper-clad chum.

The devotion ended with the singing of Mrs. Pohlmann's favorite hymn, "Blest Be the Tie that Binds." Over the next couple of school years, she had us sing it after morning devotions. Most memorably, she had us sing it for Sam, a girl from Kearsley High School who showed up weekly at the St. Mark playground and helped coach kickball. Every single time Sam left the playground, we sang whichever one of the hymn's six verses our teacher was in the mood for that day.

"Sam is leaving," Mrs. Pohlmann would announce, clapping her hands as the signal for us to encircle Sam and link arms. Verse four always seemed over the top for the occasion:

————◆ ◆————

"When here our pathways part,
We suffer bitter pain;
Yet, one in Christ and one in heart,
We hope to meet again."

—JOHN FAWCETT, 1772

————◆ ◆————

Sam must have thought we had an abnormal reverence for kickball—and a weird attachment to her.

The student at St. Mark who benefited most from my arrival was Reggie Tippit. He was a pudgy English kid whose father was in Flint training with General Motors. Reggie wore his English school uniform: navy knee-length shorts, navy knee socks, brown loafers, white Oxford shirt, navy-and-red striped necktie, navy monogrammed jacket, and a navy cap. For lunch and snack break, he brought things like leftover roast lamb, sliced beef sandwiches wrapped in wax paper and tied with twine, all manner of beets and pickles and, for dessert, some sort of tart. His lunches certainly looked more appetizing than mine—a lunch meat sandwich on Wonder Bread, an apple or orange, and a Little Debbie. Most students had the more expensive Hostess treats and individual bags of Fritos in their lunches. Reggie and I were the two kids in class without Frito Bandito erasers for our pencils. Only one classmate, Natalie, had worse lunches than mine. She refused to eat anything other than a disgusting combination of mayonnaise and mini marshmallows crushed between two slices of white bread. My snack break choice of raisins was weird *why?*

Reggie was ungainly but, to be fair, he probably had not played much softball, basketball, or kickball. When any ball was hit, thrown, or kicked his way, he bobbled, then dropped it. Most of the kids laughed at him and, in a play on his name, yelled, "Tip it, Reggie!" I admit this was, for a bunch of first and second graders, a clever turn of phrase. If Reggie had been even marginally athletic, or well-liked and self-assured, it would have been an okay chant. He was, however, none of those things.

This was the kid whose spot I took at the bottom of the social order at St. Mark. My clothes were as unfashionable as his, I was almost as bad at sports, and my Missouri accent sounded as foreign to Michiganders as did Reggie's English one. It didn't take too many days of saying I was going to "warsh" my hands before that pronunciation was jeered into oblivion.

Pecking order firmly established before the morning devotions were finished, Mrs. Pohlmann told me it was time to test my reading aptitude. She had me stand next to her desk and read aloud from the book used by the so-called average group. I had no problem with the selection from the Houghton-Mifflin reader, *Panorama*. *Fiesta* was easy, and I acquitted myself well with the selection from

Kaleidoscope, so I joined the "smart kids" group, which now consisted of me, Kurt Mann, and cutie-pie Mike Vollmer with his long
eyelashes, perfect hair, and attractive crewneck sweater. Admittance
to their group earned me grudging respect from both boys.

The remainder of my first day involved more testing to see where
I would be plugged into math and spelling, and there was a visit
with the Kearsley district nurse who came to assess my hearing and
vision. Suki La Croix (her real name, no kidding) is the reason I
have an adult terror of doctors and nurses. She was a tiny, severe
woman in her thirties with close-cropped hair, and she wore a white
uniform shirt with the band collar buttoned at her throat—similar
to the one Marcus Welby wore on television. Suki always looked
like she wanted nothing more than to deliver the tragic news to
someone that they were dying of an inoperable brain tumor, and
she loved giving shots. On this day, she observed that my hearing
was good, but I was called back for a second vision test.

"If your first test was accurate," Suki said, "then you are nearly
blind." She was visibly excited at the prospect.

Either she had done a spectacularly poor job of explaining the
eye test to me, or I was the most obtuse child ever. The eye test was
one of those where the letter E is pointing in different directions.
My job was to tell Suki if the bars of the letter were pointing up,
down, left, or right. But, when she gave me the instructions, she
told me to tell her which side the letter E was *nearest.* So, there I
was, attempting to make out some infinitesimal space between the
edges of the E and the square it was in. I thought it was an impossible task, but I'd never had my eyes tested this way before, so I did
my best. I leaned forward, straining and squinting to determine

if the E was something like 1/32 of an inch closer to the top than to the bottom. I must have looked like some cataract-plagued nonagenarian making a feeble effort to fool the DMV so I could get my license renewed.

The repeat test was administered with the teaching staff in attendance. After all, if the new pastor's daughter were going blind, it was big news! Mrs. Pohlmann asked Mr. Van Luchene, who taught third and fourth grades along with PE, to come. Naturally, he would have to know if I couldn't see a ball coming at my face during recess. Miss Hart, the music teacher, came to watch, and my dad was called from his office to bear witness to the unfolding tragedy.

There I was with an audience, again trying to discern how close that freaking E was to the edge of the square. It was the end of a day during which I'd been laughed at and whispered about and had my accent, clothing, and snack choices appraised and found wanting. I was tired and failing again at this eye test that I had no idea how *anyone* could pass. Suki, exhilarated by my potential need for a guide dog and Braille instruction, was telling my dad where I would need to go for further evaluation, when I finally reached my breaking point. I'm not so much a crier as I am a leaker. When I get angry or frustrated, my mouth scrunches up, and tears start rolling down my cheeks. Dad took one look at me and asked Suki what this "foolishness" was all about. What these people didn't yet know, but Brent and I did, was that when our father used that word, whatever activity prompting its use had better stop. Pronto.

"Tell Mrs. La Croix which way the Es are pointing," my dad gently told me.

I breezed through the test. The teachers looked relieved that they wouldn't have to make any special arrangements for my education. Suki, on the other hand, was crestfallen.

The other kids had already been dismissed for the day, so Dad came with me to my classroom and helped me put away my pencils and books. He held my hand as we walked back over the field to the parsonage. He didn't say anything at first, and he didn't ask me any questions. We walked into the house and retreated to the kitchen table with our respective modes of relaxation—mine, a glass of Kool-Aid and his, an unfiltered Camel.

"You've had a lot thrown at you today," Dad said.

I nodded, my mouth puckering and tears escaping my eyes and dripping down my chin. Mom came into the room, and she and Dad exchanged the universal "Our child is sad, and we wish we could make it better, but we can't, so we'll do our best to show her we love her" look.

"Mom, can we go look through those bags of clothes now?" I asked.

My mom, no doubt remembering the charity bin clothing she had to wear during her school years, didn't want to do that. But parenting, I've learned, is about calling audibles during unplanned moments.

"All right," she sighed, "let's go take a look."

The contents of those trash bags were what I thought I needed after my unsuccessful day at school. As I dug through them, Mom reminded me about the teasing she endured for wearing her classmates' castoffs. She counseled that wearing Kimmie's hand-me-downs might not make the transition to my new school any easier. But I couldn't or wouldn't hear her as I clutched store-bought pink corduroy bell-bottom pants. The lilac velveteen skirt with the matching vest was too dazzling for me to pay any attention to what my mom was saying. She sat on the edge of my bed, probably wishing she could wring Beverly Mann's neck.

"Okay," she yielded. "You can wear them, but if anyone, and I mean anyone, makes fun of you or calls you names, I want you to tell your father and me, and we will handle *that!*"

I gave her a solemn nod, implicit of promise, which I broke the next day after I showed up at school in one of Kimmie's flashier outfits—a bright blue mini-dress with bell sleeves and a gigantic flower print. I paired it with the white vinyl go-go boots my cousin Cheryl had given me, which, up to this point, I had worn only when playing dress-up.

Six girls from class cornered me, and their laughter came out in snorts.

"Kimmie's dress looked a lot better on her!" one said. In fairness, that was likely true.

"Charity case!" scoffed another. Was I? Technically speaking, I guess so.

"Are you a hippie?"

"Well, her hips are big enough!"

"Stupid pastor's daughter!" That one hurt the most.

Mrs. Pohlmann finally arrived in the classroom and shooed everyone to their desks. From then on, I focused on beating the mean girls the only way I knew how—by besting them on assignments and tests. By the end of the first quarter of the following school year, I had jumped ahead four grade levels in reading and spelling, and the public schools provided me with supplemental work.

I wore the hand-me-downs for another few weeks until I could no longer stomach the mocking. I folded the clothes and stored them on my closet floor, reverting to the outfits my mom had sewn for me. To her everlasting credit, Kimmie was the one girl who never teased me about wearing her former wardrobe. She acted as though she had never seen any of it. We received delivery of garment-filled trash bags from Mrs. Mann about every six months, but Mom discreetly donated them to a thrift store.

I turned seven at the end of our first full week in Flint. There were two wrapped presents on the kitchen table when I came downstairs for breakfast. One was a copy of *Little Women,* and the other was a Chinese cloth doll, about eight inches tall, dressed in a peacock and poppy tunic with matching pants and slippers. On her back, in a carrying pouch, was a similarly dressed baby boy. My mom said she had seen the doll at the dime store and bought it because she knew I liked to read about different countries and their cultures. It was a tchotchke that I loved and took pains to keep nice. Eventually, it made the move with us back to Missouri. When I married, and through moves to each of my adult homes, the doll came along. While I wouldn't in a fire stop to grab the Chinese doll, it's nice to look over at it on my bookshelf, think about the bright spot this gift was during a difficult week in my childhood, and remember that my mom wanted to give me something special.

I would have been content with the doll and book, but I was elated to find in the parsonage garage a white bike with monkey bars and a purple banana seat. The only drawback was the set of training wheels on the back. Surely, at age seven, I was the oldest kid ever to require training wheels. The day after my birthday was a Saturday, and I pedaled down the muddy street to the paved church parking lot. Thirty minutes later, Darla Nagy, who was my chief tormentor at school and lived two streets away, tooled over on her bike. There wasn't anyone else around, so she was nice to me. Darla contentedly rode around the parking lot with me for an hour until she suggested we ride over to Tracy Herbert's house. Tracy was also in our class at school. Eager to please, I agreed, and we cycled several streets over to Tracy's place where we played Barbies in her basement until I announced that I was expected home for lunch.

"Okay, bye," Darla said without looking up from where she was changing Skipper's mini-dress.

"Aren't you coming with me?" I asked.

Darla shook her head to indicate that she was not.

I was nervous. I hadn't been anywhere beyond the church property since we had moved in. I didn't know how to get back to the parsonage from Tracy's house and admitted as much.

"God will show you the way home," Tracy earnestly told me, and Darla concurred with a slow, solemn nod.

I trudged upstairs, hoping Darla would change her mind and leave with me. Instead, I heard her and Tracy's belief in divine providence collapse into a fit of giggles as they joked about how I certainly would get lost.

I recently looked online for the street configuration of our neighborhood in Flint. Other than being amazed that several streets *still* have not been paved, I see how close Tracy's house had been to the parsonage. Yet, I had been so scared that I wouldn't find my way. Also, though it had been offered without an ounce of sincerity, I took seriously Tracy's suggestion that God would help me get back to the parsonage, and I prayed out loud the entire ride. It took less than five minutes.

Over fried baloney sandwiches at lunch, I spilled the morning's chain of events to my parents. They were pleased that my first bike outing had turned out okay, but they were disappointed by Darla's behavior. I wasn't sure how to deal with her, either. She was hurtful at school and proving to be mean-spirited in the neighborhood when other kids were around. Should I stay in the house?

My dad asked me if I enjoyed riding my bike. Yes, I did. Even when unsure and frightened, I had felt an invigorating sense of freedom.

"Then keep riding," he told me. "Don't let Darla or anyone else keep you from it."

In his sermon at my wedding, Dad noted that, as a child, I had learned to orient and tell direction by church steeples. I'm sure that's what I did that day on my bike. It's what I did, literally and figuratively, during seven years in Flint with frustrating peers and teachers. During that time, Dad easily attuned his inner compass toward God, got on with things, and made the best of them. But Mom struggled. She didn't like Flint or its dank weather, yet she found a way to make life work. She taped Bible and hymn verses to the windowsill over the kitchen sink and used dishwashing time to memorize them. Back then, I thought she was a goody-goody. I'm old enough now to understand that some days cut a person off at the knees, and genuine comfort and direction can only be found in God.

Those childhood and early teen years in Flint could have been worse. I could have had parents with a poor sense of direction who didn't care what method I used to navigate life. I didn't learn on my own to tell direction from the church steeple—my mom and dad taught me that. My parents really did in all their ways acknowledge God, and He directed all our paths. Only He could make tolerable the sloppy street on which we would live for the next seven years. Because an irony-free life would be no fun at all, Daly Boulevard was finally paved, and actual curbs were installed in time for our move back to Missouri. I guess the writer of Ecclesiastes 3:11 is right about God—"He has made everything beautiful in its time."

Chapter Eleven

Open the Door and See All the People

St. Mark Lutheran Church, Flint,
Michigan, c. 1973

Flint, Michigan, along with St. Mark Lutheran congregation and its members, impacted me for life. Our Flint church family influenced my faith more than any other, probably because I was in those impressionable years from ages seven to fourteen when a kid notices and absorbs the world. I found most of the people in our congregation and neighborhood fascinating in ways that were either admirable or peculiar.

My dad faced his greatest vocational demands in Flint. A day school always makes congregational life more challenging, and when a pastor inherits an enterprise that gained voter assembly approval by one slim vote, as happened at St. Mark, he is stuck dealing with two factions with opposite goals: "We need more money" versus "close the school." Add to the mix the roller coaster fortunes of the local economy, with people going from earning good United Auto Workers wages to being laid off, and sometimes the congregation barely eked out enough money from offerings to pay salaries and utility bills. Dad enjoyed the demands of his ministry in Flint, but they took a toll on him, and he sought relief in three ways: smoking, gardening, and ice fishing.

Dad kicked up his two-packs-per-day habit to three packs in Flint. Because this was before Mom banned him from smoking indoors, the rest of us benefited from his unfiltered Camels, too. One of the few times Dad didn't smoke was when he worked in his garden. We had a garden at every parsonage, but in Flint the harvest kept not only our family but also the neighbors and much of the congregation well-supplied with vegetables. Dad started out with a patch at the parsonage that measured roughly 200 square feet, which is good-sized but relatively small compared to his garden in Liberty.

What led to the exponential increase in yield was my parents' purchase of ten acres of land east of Flint. I assumed that meant they were going to build a house and we would move there. My suspicions increased when Mom, anxious for decorating ideas, dragged me with her to visit model homes. Tired of neighborhood life already because of Darla Nagy, I was overjoyed at the prospect of moving to a spot where I could act like my literary heroines, Anne Shirley and Jo March. I resolved to climb in the property's overgrown apple trees, bike down the dusty dirt road, and splash in the creek that ran along the north border of the property. The adjacent piece of land belonged to the Frost family from church. Hal and Trix and their three daughters lived in a three-bedroom ranch on their ten acres. Sociable and fun-loving, they regularly invited us for dinner. The girls were so happy when they found out we had purchased the neighboring acreage that they built a primitive bridge over the creek as a shortcut between our respective parcels. My parents, however, had to save up enough money to build, and in the intervening years Hal and Trix divorced and sold their home. Meanwhile, my mom was growing increasingly disappointed with Michigan weather and anxious about the number of cigarettes Dad was smoking.

We never moved from the parsonage, but my dad planted a huge garden every year on "the land." I went with him several days a week every summer to pull weeds and pick vegetables. He had the usual tomatoes and corn, and now there was room for eggplant, turnips, kohlrabi, spinach, broccoli, beets, and manifold varieties of squash that forced my mom to find new and unappealing recipes for their use. After giving away 80 percent of the crop, we still had bushelsful for ourselves. Mom canned her usual hundreds of jars of tomatoes and added seventy quarts each of dill and sweet pickles each summer. Our garage floor was lined all June and July with antique Red Wing crocks filled with cucumbers and brining solution, each one topped with a plate to keep out dirt. After the pickles were canned, we snacked on them, added them to sandwiches, and, best of all, placed them atop soda crackers spread with liverwurst. Mom's sweet pickles were amazing, but her dill pickles, though good, did not keep Dad and me from a desire for the store-bought version, especially Michigan-grown Vlasic pickles.

"Can't we just get one jar?" I whined when we passed the kosher dills at the supermarket. "Just one this *one* time?"

My mom was unmoved.

"Karen Ann," she began, "we are not going to spend good money on dill pickles when we have seventy jars of them at home."

If my dad happened to be along on the shopping trip, he would shoot me a sympathetic glance. He liked the Vlasic dill pickles better, too, but had the good sense to keep quiet about it. When I was nine years old and, yet again, rifling through Dad's desk, I discovered his secret. He had a jar of his favorite Vlasic Polish dills hidden in the bottom right drawer. The next time we had a private moment, I confronted him.

"I found the pickles in your desk, Dad," leveling the accusation with as much disapproval as if I had found a stash of weed.

He hesitated before answering. "Let's not tell your mother," he said. "I don't want to hurt her feelings." I didn't buy this for a minute. Her feelings wouldn't have been hurt—Dad didn't want to deal with the fallout. My mom could deliver a lecture on frugality and wastefulness like nobody else.

"Okay." I stood there, waiting for Dad to accept my unspoken bribe.

"All right," he said. "You can have some of my Vlasics, but we have to keep eating at least some of your mother's pickles." We had a deal. Years later, when my parents had more money, and my mom had wearied of canning, she voluntarily stocked the pantry with Vlasic pickles. They weren't nearly as delicious as the contraband ones had been.

During the long Flint winters, with no garden to mitigate the stress of his duties, Dad needed something to do on Fridays, his ostensible day off. He was thrilled when Harold Yurk introduced him to ice fishing. Every Friday, Dad piled his gear into the bed of Harold's harvest-gold pickup truck, and they headed ninety miles north of Flint to Saginaw Bay on Lake Huron. When he first started ice fishing, my dad's equipment consisted of the tiny pole ice fishers use, a five-pound coffee can full of charcoal briquettes, and his shabby, everyday overcoat. When ice on the bay was solid, and probably ten inches thick, Mr. Yurk drove his truck onto the frozen surface. It was safe to do this, but Mom insisted my dad not return the favor by driving *our* car onto the ice. After using an auger to drill fishing holes, the two men lit the charcoal briquettes, warmed their hands, and drank coffee or schnapps when they weren't removing perch, pike, or walleye from the ends of their lines. I don't recall Dad ever mentioning a catch limit, and it was not unusual for him and Harold to return to Flint with hundreds of fish between them.

Once back at the parsonage, Dad spread newspaper on the concrete basement floor, dumped the frozen fish from the coolers he used to store his catch, and unboxed his wicked filet knife. Initially,

I was under strict orders never to go near the knife, but before long, I persuaded Dad to teach me how to clean, gut, and filet a fish. He was a fast worker—a necessity because the fish weren't dead. Once thawed, they writhed on the floor, making it more difficult to cut off their heads without also slicing off a finger. I was allowed to thaw one fish in the laundry sink so I could watch it swim before it, too, was decapitated. By 9:00 p.m., Dad had fileted, packaged, and put into our chest freezer dozens of pounds of perch and was looking forward to his next trip.

Harold was Dad's most consistent fishing buddy, but they also invited others along. Marv Herzog, Michigan's polka king, often accompanied them to Saginaw Bay. Mr. Herzog was based in Frankenmuth, a charming German town north of Flint famous for Bronner's Christmas store, The Bavarian Inn, Zehnder's Restaurant, and, of course, Marv Herzog. Following his stint in the military, Marv returned home to Frankenmuth, formed a polka band, and started playing at fairs and festivals around the state. Marv developed a loyal following, and his fan club numbered in the thousands. We had eight-track recordings of his hits, including "Im Himmel da gibt's kein Bier," "Eins, Zwei, Drei, G'Suffa," "Beer Barrel Polka," and "I Don't Want Her, You Can Have Her, She's Too Fat for Me." Dad going ice fishing with Marv Herzog was a fusion of Michigan music and sport akin to somebody today going bowhunting with Ted Nugent.

Marv, Harold, and my dad were companionable ice fishing buddies, but complications ensued when two other pastors, Wally Marth and Emil Klausen, came along. Pastor Klausen was from Minnesota, but his speech suggested that he had, in the last few weeks, emigrated from Norway. Like any group of guys, the fishermen sometimes used first or last names in reference to each other. So, along with Harold Yurk, there was my dad, Marv; Marv Herzog; Pastor Marth; and Pastor Klausen who, with his accent, didn't pronounce either "v" or "th" with distinction. It was "Marf, Marf, Marf, Marf, Marf" all day long, and misunderstandings arose. "Marf had the auger," "Marf drank all the schnapps," "Marf doesn't want to give the devotion at the next pastors' conference." It was the Lutheran pastor version of "Who's on First," and Pastor Marth was sick of it.

"Who are you talking about?" he yelled—*really* yelled, according to my dad, who was not prone to exaggeration. "MarV or MarTH?—and which MarV?" To be fair, everybody knew Marv Herzog wasn't trying to shirk the devotion, but it could have been anyone who misplaced the auger or polished off the schnapps. Pastor Marth wanted some clarity, dammit!

It was a quiet drive back to Flint. My dad brokered a tenuous peace between gentle Pastor Klausen and forthright Pastor Marth, but they remained, respectively, hurt and surly, and it was probably uncomfortable for the non-pastors to see them on the outs. This was nothing new for my dad, though, as he was a regular participant in the most combative of all activities among Lutheran clergy in Flint: Thursday volleyball.

Dad loved the twice-monthly matches. He had been a decent high school athlete, particularly in track. His high hurdles record stood for decades, and he was a decent basketball player with two equally competitive brothers, so spiking the ball in the face of a fellow pastor would not have been a problem for him. The other pastors were similarly aggressive—think Ben Stiller's unfortunate spike in *Meet the Parents* (minus the Speedos, thank goodness).

Volleyball was also a way for the pastors to size up their vicars. For several of the supervising pastors in Flint, the assigned vicars may have had oratorical talent and compassion in spades, but if they wimped out on the volleyball court, they were found wanting.

My dad had lucked out with his vicar, Keith Ratcliffe—a congenial and scrappy young guy who had grown up poor in Detroit. Unlike Bob Kranz's vicar, Keith kept his head down and his opinions to himself. Pastor Kranz, my favorite of all the pastors in Flint, was a solid, swarthy man, and incredibly friendly, but he was the most competitive of the group. These volleyball matches were scored and officiated on the honor system, and, confident of each other's integrity, no one ever disputed a call. One day, Bob Kranz's vicar didn't attempt to return a serve, so the other team was awarded a point. The vicar challenged the point, arguing the ball had been served out of bounds. The pastors on his team disagreed, but the vicar kept at it, holding up the match and irritating everyone. Finally, Pastor Kranz stormed over to the guy and, two inches from his face, screamed, "Shut up! You're just a vicar!"

When Dad told this story over dinner that evening, my mom was shocked that Bob Kranz had treated his vicar so harshly. My dad assured her it had been for the best. All year, the kid had been hectoring Pastor Kranz about "the right way to serve"—and not in the volleyball sense. He was vocal at pastors' conferences, too, lecturing the experienced pastors about the spiritually correct way to do things.

"He's not too keen on work, either," my dad said about the vicar. Dad had a theory—one I've observed over the years to be accurate. He believed a vicar's, and many a pastor's, work ethic was inversely proportional to how much that person talked about loving and serving the Lord. For example, one of my dad's subsequent vicars announced he could not make hospital or shut-in calls because he wanted to use his vicarage solely for Bible study and prayer. My dad didn't have a bad temper, but I would have paid big-time cash to see the look on his face when his vicar told him that. I'm certain he leveled his ice-blue eyes at the guy and calmly said something like, "You will pay a visit to Mrs. Schmidt at Beautiful Savior nursing home before noon today." It would have been implicit that if this did not happen, the guy should pack his bags and head back to his hometown, his shot at the ministry torpedoed by his own laziness.

Our family frequently hung out with both the Marth and Klausen families, each of which had several kids. Bobby Klausen was my age, and everybody thought he was a genius, so I didn't like him. Once, when we all were over at the parsonage where the Marths lived, Bobby was holding forth about his favorite dinosaur, diplodocus. Only the moms and kids were in the room—the dads were on the patio grilling burgers and smoking. Bobby's sister Ruth, Becky Marth, and I were getting bored, so we tried to escape, but our mothers told us to sit and listen to Bobby.

"He has ten dinosaurs to go," his mom said. Crap.

Eileen Klausen, slightly younger than my mom but far stricter, quoted scripture to keep her kids in line. If, say, her youngest child, Esther, grabbed Ruth's Holly Hobbie doll and Ruth complained, Mrs. Klausen was ready with a Bible verse.

"Ruth, remember, 'Do not forget to do good and to share, for, with such sacrifices, God is well pleased.'" That's from the book of Hebrews—chapter thirteen, verse sixteen. Mrs. Klausen was a drag.

My mom, however, thought she was great. She told Dad and me how Eileen was once so fed up with Pastor Klausen being gone for meetings that she called their church secretary and asked her to pencil in an appointment with the pastor. Eileen dressed in her Sunday best, walked over to the church from their parsonage, and told her husband that this was the only way to get his attention. Thereafter, they would have a weekly appointment at church.

"Isn't that wonderful?" Mom exclaimed. "She even wore a hat and gloves."

I wasn't impressed. "I think it sounds stupid."

My dad, probably hoping my mom wouldn't pull a similar stunt, agreed with me. He found the hat and gloves bit especially ridiculous. "What was she trying to prove with that?"

Mom admired cleanliness, exemplary behavior, and piety. Eileen Klausen and her children were the total package.

"Marvin, you know how talented Bobby is," she said. "He knows all the dinosaurs, and so much of the Bible like his mother does!"

My dad, who did not go around spouting Bible verses to suit an occasion, paraphrased one now. I had to look up the words to discover they were from Acts 4:13.

"The disciples were uneducated," Dad responded. "But people knew they had been with Jesus."

My mom was unmoved. "Well, I don't know about *that!*" she said. "But, I do know how smart Bobby is!"

"And life isn't a show," Dad said. "Quoting the Bible isn't a competition, and your children are as intelligent as Bobby." Bam! Dad 1—Eileen Klausen 0.

Pastors' families often socialized in Flint. There were summer picnics and winter potluck dinners, and my parents went out for pizza and beer one Friday night per month with their best friends, Pastor and Mrs. Cario. Once a month, couples took turns hosting the Pastors' Party—a gathering for all the Flint circuit pastors and their wives. (A "circuit" is a geographic division. Just as the United States is composed of counties, states, and regions, the Missouri Synod is made up of circuits, zones, and districts.)

Children were persona non grata at these parties, except for those living at the host parsonage who were to be seen but not heard and adept at keeping the snacks coming. My parents allowed me to tend bar when it was their turn to host. I served beer from the pony keg and mixed all the drinks—mostly Manhattans, Tom Collins, and Scotch neat. Mom bought the cheapest bottle of Scotch they had at Haden's Market on Genesee Road. I'm guessing it tasted like death. In between filling drink orders, I watched and listened. It was a tradition at the party that, upon arrival, men and women split into separate groups. This was still the era when pastors and their wives were warned against developing friendships within a congregation, so this opportunity to be just another guy or gal was prized among the pastoral couples.

The men talked shop in the basement while the women vented in the living room—Eileen Klausen complaining loudest and longest about her role as helpmeet to her husband. To my mom's absolute credit, she never joined in the complaints—she wasn't a gossip. It was enough for her to listen and be assured that other women also had to put up with hard-to-please church members and a perpetually absent husband.

Equally as predictable as Mrs. Klausen's lamentations were Dot Schneider's health rants. She ate no snacks and drank nothing but water. She wore no makeup and hated food and beverage conglomerates. If she's still alive, I imagine she is leading the charge against factory farms, Big Pharma, and whatever company makes those chemical-laden frozen snacks my son eats by the dozen.

"Carbonated drinks cause cancer," she lectured, rattling off statistics about all the rats and mice that died from ingesting the stuff. "You are killing your kids if you let them drink pop."

The other women nodded in agreement as they puffed their cigarettes.

The Bittlers were the most intriguing couple at the parties. They were former missionaries who recently had returned stateside. Pastor Bittler was a brawny guy with a bear-hug friendliness, and his wife wore short skirts with boots and kept her hair long instead of combed and set like the other ladies. Their stories about missionary work were captivating, but I worried when my parents showed what I thought was too much interest, fearing *they* were considering serving overseas. Then I overheard a conversation between the Bittlers and my dad about their difficult re-entry to the United States. They and their children had come from a happy life in Africa back to the most enticing candy store of a country there ever was, and the adjustment was taking a toll on their marriage and family. I was a typical, empathy-challenged pre-teen so, instead of feeling compassion for this struggling family like I ought to have, I was glad their life was proving to be a cautionary tale against mission work.

In addition to church members and fellow pastors seeking my dad's counsel, neighbors often did, too. They never went to Gil Cutler, the fussy pastor of the Assemblies of God church catty-corner from us on Genesee Road. Maybe everybody thought he was strange because he loved nothing better in his spare time than to drive his riding lawn mower around his yard every single spring, summer, and fall day while wearing a dress shirt and pants. This worried my mother as she imagined his wife having difficulty getting grass stains out of her husband's Haggar slacks.

Maybe, to the neighbors, my dad seemed like a regular guy who could be of practical, as well as spiritual, help when they needed it. One lady on our street, Mrs. Polinski, showed up in hysterics at the parsonage one evening. Mom invited her inside, and she and Dad tried to calm her and ascertain what was wrong.

"I'm having surgery next week," she said. "I don't know if I'll make it."

My parents exchanged concerned looks, and Dad promised to visit the woman in the hospital. He asked if she felt comfortable telling him about the nature of her problem, probably hoping it didn't have anything to do with the reproductive system. My dad was, by this time, desensitized to scars, incisions, rashes, and gunshot wounds, but "female problems" were something about which he wanted no details.

Our wailing neighbor asked Dad to sit with her husband during her surgery in case she didn't survive, and she finally disclosed that the procedure entailed . . . resetting two bones in her hand. I heard volumes in my parents' silence as they weighed Mrs. Polinski's behavior against her relatively innocuous condition. She came to the parsonage at least a dozen times over seven years.

"Dad," I yelled downstairs one evening after answering the door to find, once again, our distraught neighbor. "Mrs. Polinski wants to talk to you!"

I wasn't sure he had heard me, but then I heard him sigh, "Oh, brother." By the time he arrived upstairs, he had put on his game face and looked like he wanted nothing more than to help our neighbor. I was by then old enough to get that my parents regularly gave up most of their time to deal with other peoples' issues (or, in this case, non-issues), so I gave my dad a "this sucks for you" look. He nodded in agreement before trying, once more, to provide some consolation.

The parsonage property backed up to the McKays' yard. They were an older couple who ignored our family for four years until they called my dad when their daughter was hospitalized for a ruptured appendix. Suzette recovered, and, from that night on, the McKays couldn't do enough for our family. Helen and David, we discovered, were from the United Kingdom. Suddenly, their distant demeanors made sense—they were British. Helen invited Mom and me to afternoon tea and served us a spread of delicacies: cucumber sandwiches, scones, clotted cream, lemon curd, and, best of all, trifle. I felt like I was in a scene from a novel about the English upper class, sipping my tea and daydreaming about ball gowns when Mr. McKay, completely naked and smoking a pipe, walked into the room. My mom was startled and embarrassed, and I tried not to laugh. I didn't know a living person could be that pale.

"David McKay," Helen scolded, "go put some clothes on!" She turned to us and asked, "You don't mind that he was naked, do you?"

Mom elbowed me so I would stop gawking at Mr. McKay's retreating posterior and laughed to cover her discomfort. I could not wait to get home to tell Dad about teatime.

Because we had enjoyed the trifle so much, Helen brought us one every week. By the eighth week, we were tiring of it. After six months, we couldn't eat another trifle. That's when my mom hatched what I, in retrospect, think was a clever plan.

"Helen," my mom said as she reached for yet another bowl of the offering from our neighbor. "It's so wonderful of you to make this for us, but Karen is *dying* to learn how to make one herself." I was standing right there when she said this, and I can tell you that I was *not* dying to learn how to make a trifle, but I was willing to see where this was going. "Maybe you could share your recipe with her so she can make *you* one, for once."

Mrs. McKay was ecstatic. She wrote out the recipe for me but warned I couldn't make a trifle with any old ingredients from an American grocery store. Her UK relatives regularly shipped her boxes of Bird's Custard Powder along with sponge fingers and proper English raspberry jam. From then on, she would have them send double the amount so that I could have my own authentic ingredients. Helen's foodstuff deliveries were as faithful as her trifles had been. Mom had not seen this coming, and she didn't want to hurt our neighbor's feelings, so every few weeks, she made sure I assembled a trifle that we forced ourselves to eat. It was a small price to pay for the continued neighborliness with the British McKays who, like most German people I've known, were at first reticent to the point of standoffishness but, once acquainted, couldn't do enough to demonstrate kindness.

✶

Throughout my dad's ministry, he and Mom were perennially cheerful givers. My brother and I knew without being lectured that giving to God was paramount. Sharing with others was also imperative, although my parents had to learn to be cheerful receivers, too. In Westgate, for instance, a farmer showed up one day at the parsonage and handed a bag of apples to Dad.

"I was going to feed these to the pigs," the farmer said, "but then I thought of you."

Okay, *that* anecdote might not demonstrate generosity, exactly. But people at each of the congregations my dad served did demonstrate uncommon liberality, and the folks in Flint kicked it up several notches.

One example of this benevolence was the free eye care given to our family by Dr. Visser. The first time Mom and I went for eye exams, he confidentially told her all our exams, lenses, and frames would be gratis for as long as we lived in Flint. My mom, of course, tried to talk him out of this, but he prevailed. He was thrilled to do this for his pastor's family. Now that I have to write the check for glasses and contact lenses, I understand what a phenomenal gift this was. The only downside was that when it came time to select my frames, my mom looked for the cheapest ones. Naturally, the least expensive pair was also the least attractive.

"Be grateful, Karen Ann!" Mom scolded *before I had even complained* about my frames.

"I didn't say anything!"

"You were thinking it," she replied. Clearly, if she knew what I was thinking, then she also knew they were ugly. In fairness, Mom searched out the cheapest frames for herself, too. And it was the 1970s, so 95 percent of them were hideous anyway.

Also atrocious in the 1970s were crocheted beer can hats—the ones with bright yarn and cut-outs from cans of Budweiser and Pabst Blue Ribbon. I was surprised to discover that these hats are still being made, having found an online tutorial for their construction. "Be prepared for everyone to comment on your one-of-a-kind creation at your next house party,"[1] the accompanying statement warns.

Hazel Fuchs regularly worshipped with her son Jonathan, who also attended school at St. Mark. Hazel was a divorcee, still a rarity among Lutherans in the 1970s. Fourteen-year-old Jon was cute in a *Tiger Beat* kind of way with his long, feathered hair and soft facial features. He usually paired his bell bottoms with flowing, puffy shirts.

Mrs. Fuchs loved to crochet, and she made scores of beer and Sun-Glo pop can hats. (The world of Michigan carbonated beverages was dominated by Vernors ginger ale and Faygo and Sun-Glo soda pops. Sun-Glo was the least expensive, so that's what Mom bought.) Every fall for the congregational harvest dinner and bazaar, Hazel had a table of hats for sale. One Christmas, she gave my parents matching Budweiser hats and scarves, leading me to wonder how much warmth could be provided by something made from aluminum cans. The following January, I asked my mom in all sincerity why she wasn't wearing her hat and scarf. She shot me a look that said, "I'm never wearing them, I'll never allow your father to wear his, and you will keep that information to yourself, young lady."

Mrs. Fuchs was the only woman at St. Mark who wore a hat to church—a regular hat, not a beer hat. She adhered rigidly to the words in I Corinthians that said women should, for the purpose of modesty, cover their heads. Head-covering for women is a non-issue in our denomination. Those, like my mom, who wore hats usually did so because they were in style, and most women in the Missouri Synod ditched theirs when they were no longer trendy. But Hazel Fuchs took the matter seriously. She often talked with my dad about the disturbing lack of rules at church, and she wanted him to institute a policy requiring women to wear hats for worship. Dad probably felt sorry for her, knowing she was shackling herself to an unnecessary burden. Judging from what she did one Sunday, she thought my dad was a heretic.

I'm still uncomfortable when I think about what happened that summer morning. I perceived the incident as an attack on my dad, and in that moment, I despised Mrs. Fuchs. I was twelve—old enough to sense the tension but too young to understand it. About five minutes into the sermon, Hazel left her usual pew on the north side of the sanctuary and marched to the pulpit. She began shouting at my dad, quoting Bible verses, and adding commentary. When she finished, she yelled "Fine!" before untying the ribbons on her hat and throwing it on the floor. She strode out of the church, not even looking at Jonathan, who sat shell-shocked in their pew. He stood and followed her, and I heard him wail, "Why did you have to do that?" My dad had remained impassive during Hazel's outburst, and when she left, he continued with his sermon. I glanced at my mom, and she was crying. She, too, was disturbed on my dad's behalf, or so I thought. Everybody was stunned, and several other women were crying.

Sunday dinner at the parsonage was subdued. I was confused by Mrs. Fuch's tirade and upset for my dad. My feelings remained unaltered even after my parents explained Mrs. Fuchs was going through a rough time, and that had caused her to lash out. They ordinarily would not reveal private information to me, but they knew I needed an honest explanation and trusted me to keep quiet. When I suggested my mom also was angry, offering her tears as proof, she told me she felt terrible for Hazel, not my dad. Dad wasn't upset, but he was quiet.

"Marvin, several people wondered why you continued with your sermon," Mom said.

"What else was there to do?" he asked her, clearly weary. "It's not that easy." I thought then that he was talking about his sermon, but now I know he meant being a pastor and dealing with people and their stuff.

It took a couple of years, but Mrs. Fuchs came back to church— sans hat. I don't remember Jon being with her. I didn't realize it then, but of all the people in church the morning of his mother's rant, he took the hardest hit. I hope there was as much reconciliation between him and his mom as there was between Hazel and her church family, her pastor, and, above all, her Savior Who promises rest for the heavily burdened and Who knows the number of hairs on our heads—covered or uncovered.

As famous as Hazel Fuchs was for her crocheted beer can hats, Ginette Graubner was known for her extraordinary homemade outfits. She made clothes for her entire family, including suits for her husband and jeans for her two teenage sons. My mom was impressed with Ginette's skills.

"Marvin, I would *never* make you a suit," Mom declared one morning at breakfast.

"I think that's best for everyone," Dad said. He knew she had the chops to do a good job, but her perfectionism put stress on us all.

My favorite Ginette Graubner originals were the matching pant suits she made for her family. The white, wide-lapel jackets and flare-leg pants were paired with black pinstripe shirts, and a black pocket square completed each ensemble. The Graubners could have passed for mobsters or pimps but, because they unselfconsciously embraced their attire, no one batted an eye.

As remarkable as the Graubners' regular Sunday outfits were, even they lacked the wow factor of Ginette's most daring creation—a dress for the U.S. Bicentennial, July 4, 1976, which fell on a Sunday. Keeping it secret from everyone but her husband and my dad, Mrs. Graubner had sewn a fantastic patriotic dress to celebrate her country's two-hundredth birthday. She wanted it to be a surprise to Dad, too, but shared her plan with him to ensure she wouldn't be a distraction that morning, particularly during communion.

Ginette Graubner was radiant as she walked up the aisle that Sunday, accompanied by her husband, who sported lavender velveteen knee breeches and a matching colonial-style frock coat, stockings, buckle shoes, a silky white shirt, and a tricorn hat. But he was no match for his wife, who wore the biggest, brightest flag of a dress anyone there had ever seen. It was striped and starred and featured side bustles so wide that she took up enough space for four people at the altar railing. Her hair was coiffed to towering effect. She was Betsy Ross meets Marie Antoinette.

Too many Missouri Synod Lutherans behave as if solemnity equals reverence, and consequently we appear as though we are headed for lethal injection when we take communion. But Ginette didn't look like she was headed to her death that day. She had the jubilant expression of a sinner who is receiving life and forgiveness at the Lord's table. Hers was a dual celebration of the American revolution against British tyranny and Christ's revolution against sin, death, and the power of the Devil. And it was magnificent.

Chapter Twelve

The Win Column

Aspiring author and victim of bullying
by loud plaid and synthetic fur,
Flint, Michigan, 1977

A side from the adults in Flint whose generosity and eccentricities influenced and entertained me, there were two kids my age who also, for better or worse, made an impact: Brenda Nowak, whom I never actually met, but with whom I had a one-sided, competitive relationship; and Darla, my neighborhood nemesis.

I encountered Brenda through the "Wide Awake Club," a weekly spread in *The Flint Journal* that showcased poems, drawings, jokes, and short prose submitted by kids hoping for publication and, perhaps, a prize. I first noticed the feature when I was ten years old. The drawings and jokes didn't interest me, but the poetry and short stories did, especially the work of Brenda Nowak, age twelve. She ruled the "Wide Awake Club" in the mid-1970s, having several pieces published every week. I was acutely jealous of her because I, too, had literary aspirations.

I had already published several editions of my own neighborhood newspaper, *The Daly News*—a nod to our muddy street's name. Printed by hand on notebook paper, my articles featured items of local interest such as the Polinskis' new car and Lily Benjamin's dead cat. Because drafting by hand was tedious, only a couple copies circulated each week. My best story was about Anna Hinkel, who lived down the street. Mrs. Hinkel had been born in Germany and, as a teenager, was interred in a Soviet prison camp along with her mother toward the end of World War II. After the war ended, they were released, and ten years later, Anna met her husband Ken, an American GI stationed in Germany. He brought her to the United States, and Anna fell in love with her new country. She graciously agreed to an interview in her home.

"We were starving," Mrs. Hinkel explained as I sat next to a table laden, as per German tradition for entertaining even one visitor, with five cakes. "We had soup sometimes, but the Russian soldiers enjoyed putting out their cigarettes in it."

I was too young to know what else Soviet soldiers enjoyed doing to captive German women, so her story of tobacco-tainted food sounded to me like the height of suffering. After fielding several of my naïve questions, Anna packaged some cake for my family and me, and I headed home to write. The headline, neatly written in pencil on paper that was still rough-edged where I'd hastily torn it from my spiral notebook, proclaimed, "World War Two Was Really Bad for One Woman." I copied an extra sheet and told my mom I was taking it to Mrs. Hinkel. She didn't think that was a good idea.

"Why can't I go show her?" I was near tears.

"Karen Ann," Mom said. "*Really.*"

"Really, *what?*" I was full-on crying now.

She put her hands on her hips and looked at me, expecting me to give in.

"Dad," I yelled down to the study where he was working. "Come up here!"

It was to my advantage that my dad didn't enjoy seeing me cry. We were not a family that publicly expressed emotion, but in private I was incredibly in touch with my feelings.

"Mom says I can't show Mrs. Hinkel my article," I explained between ugly gulps.

"Why not?" Dad asked.

"*Marvin,*" was my mom's short answer. Her longer and, let's be honest here, more accurate answer would have been, "because it's awful."

"She's been working hard on this."

"But I don't want Anna to think—" Mom didn't get to finish.

"She'll think it's a nice piece of work," Dad said, turning to me. "Go show it to her."

Mrs. Hinkel liked the story—all twelve lines. It was probably the shallowest narrative ever written about the aftermath of World

War II, but she was glad that someone had taken the time to tell her story, and I returned to my Mom with an air of "I told you so."

There were things I didn't understand about my mom until I became a parent, and by then she had died. She was in my brain, though, when my son's elementary school ambition was to play in the NBA, and I wanted to warn him of the statistical improbability of his dream coming true. My mom played it safe, both for herself and her children, and I didn't want to carry on the tradition. So, I encouraged my son, who practiced ball control on the driveway until the basketball was an extension of his body, using my dad's voice: "You've given this a lot of effort—go show them what you've got."

I had to work up the nerve to submit something to the "Wide Awake Club," and when I was at last ready to face rejection or ridicule, I waited until there was a good topic of the week. Brenda Nowak might have been willing to waste her time on subject matter like clowns or kittens, but I certainly wasn't. When the notice of submission for the topic "Seasons" appeared, I grabbed my trusty spiral notebook and worked hard for half an hour. When I was satisfied with my scribblings, I ripped out the page, stuffed it into a hastily addressed envelope, and gave it to my dad to mail. Then I waited three weeks until the publication of "Seasons."

I watched from the front porch for the paper boy. My parents were continuously aggravated that this kid couldn't get the paper on the driveway to save his life. (On a rather Dickensian note, no one in the neighborhood knew his name. He was the Paper Boy— disheveled and unhappy.) Finally! Before he could toss the *Journal* into the bushes, I grabbed it from him, ran inside, and flopped down on the family room floor to look for my poem.

My parents pretended nonchalance as I scanned through drawings of autumn leaves and jokes about winter, hoping to see my name. There was an anecdote about changing seasons by Brenda Nowak, but she wasn't listed as a weekly winner. And there it was: "Spring" by Karen Kuhlmann. Honorable mention—not a win, but it was close! I screamed. Mom screamed, and Dad jumped from his chair.

"Well?" they both demanded.

"I got an honorable mention!"

Because neither parent had read my poem, I handed over the paper so they could enjoy what, in retrospect, was a uniformly awful ode to blossoms and sunshine. Judging from my parents' reactions, however, one would think I had mapped the human genome. Dad drove to Haden's Market to buy extra copies of the paper so Mom could mail my poem to relatives. I had such a sweet feeling of success that I never again submitted to the "Wide Awake Club." I had achieved my two-pronged goal: get published and beat Brenda Nowak.

The one person I could never best was Darla Nagy. When she wasn't pushing me into mud puddles or plowing into me while I rode my bike, she was engineering selfish Barbie scenarios in which she had exclusive use of her Barbie car while I made do with an empty tissue box. Her Ken had a management position at the Ternstedt division of GM while my Ken had to be either a pastor or a janitor. Sometimes we played that our Kens were the ambulance-driving guys from *Emergency*. Her Ken was always cute Randy Mantooth, and mine was the less desirable Kevin Tighe. Meanwhile, Darla insisted on being able to use my Barbie clothing—gorgeous evening gowns and sporty separates my mom had sewn for me.

The Nagy family was incredibly dysfunctional and often engaged in spectacular screaming matches. They also kept a loaf of bread next to the cat's litter box in their bathroom.

"Have some bread if you want!" Darla yelled to me as I sat emptying my bladder.

"That's okay!" I yelled back.

She kept the bathroom door open when she went, munching on a piece of Wonder Bread. I shook my head "no" when she held out a slice to me after she wiped. Any sort of food/bathroom combination still bothers me forty-odd years later.

I was Darla's BFF when it was only the two of us, but if anyone else showed up, her demeanor changed instantly. Her mother liked it that her daughter was top dog; I overhead her saying so to another parent at school. My parents begged me to stop playing with Darla, but I craved friendship, and it beat staying inside to help my mom iron.

The summer I was eleven wasn't too bad, primarily due to the unexpected and unexplained arrival of Friend. I think she was my age, but that's a guess because no one knew anything about her. She just appeared one day. I didn't know where she lived, but she started hanging out with me every day. My memory tells me that her name may have been Lisa or Tracy, but I only called her Friend. *She* only called herself Friend. She looked like the archetypal girl-book protagonist: freckled, brown hair in pigtails, white t-shirt, shorts, and tennis shoes with laces undone. She liked to eat the hard, unripe pears from the tree at the back of the parsonage. Because Friend was more about action than Barbies, we raced bikes during the day and caught fireflies or played midnight bloody murder after dark.

"Who is that girl, Karen Ann?" my mom asked a few days after Friend started showing up at our backyard picnic table every morning.

"Friend," I answered.

"What do you mean, *Friend?*"

"That's her name," I informed her.

"It is not!" she informed me back.

We went on like this for several minutes, Mom grilling me about the identity and provenance of Friend and me unable to provide answers. To be fair, if a strange kid showed up at my house now, calling himself "Pal" and picking vegetables from my garden, I'd be wary, too. Mom ultimately acknowledged Friend was a nice girl and willingly shared our Kool-Aid popsicles with her. Unfortunately, once school started, Friend disappeared, and it was back to Darla, who continued to taunt me about my clothes, my weight, my hair, and my loser persona. Although most of her mocking and bullying was wholly unjustified, there was one instance when I had it coming.

When Darla had her ears pierced, she came over to the parsonage to show them off. My mom, in front of Darla, sternly reminded me that I had to wait until I was sixteen for pierced ears. At school the next day, Darla told the girls assembled in the restroom how much of a hardass my mom was. Her impersonation of my mother was credible enough that it hurt my heart. That's when I said something unbelievably stupid.

"I'm getting my ears pierced," I told the group.

Darla wheeled on me. "You are not!"

"Yes, I am." If I had left it at that, I would have salvaged a sliver of dignity and bought myself some time. But my opponent was vastly superior to me, and she knew it.

"I'm going to ask your parents tonight, and you'll get in trouble for lying."

So much of childhood is verbal combat—assessing the skill of your adversary, taking stock of your own arsenal, then laying down the assault. Unfortunately, I was a green buck private, and Darla was Patton. If I'd taken a moment to strategize, I would have known that had she shown up at the parsonage asking questions, my parents would have told her to go home. They gave no quarter to busybodies, particularly bratty pre-teen ones. So, instead of considering my parents' inscrutability and loyalty, I made a tactical blunder.

"They won't be home tonight," I said. "Because we're going to get my ears pierced."

"Reeeeeaaaallly?" Darla knew this was bogus. "I can't wait to see them tomorrow, right guys?" she asked the gaggle of antagonistic Lutheran schoolgirls. A few seemed willing to give me the benefit of the doubt, but Terri Abel and Sissy Davis looked smug and triumphant.

Although I readily shared my opinions with my parents, I never easily shared feelings of sadness or fear. I could have mitigated my idiocy by telling them about my predicament, and they would have given me good advice. And who knows? They both disliked Darla enough that my mom might have reversed her rule on piercing.

But, instead of turning to my parents for help, I spent the evening scouring the parsonage for a solution. I looked through my dad's desk, his tool and tackle boxes, and Mom's sewing box before I took note of the beer Dad was drinking. I searched the trash can for his discarded ring-tab, then went to the refrigerator, grabbed a Sun-Glo lemon-lime pop, and pocketed that ring-tab, too. In my bedroom, I snapped off the rings and bent the tabs in half. They clamped perfectly onto my earlobes. To my delusional pre-adolescent brain, my ears looked so authentically pierced that I didn't dare go downstairs for fear my mom would believe I'd taken a needle and done the deed myself, so I stayed in my room and planned my outfit for the next day. I decided my earrings would be best highlighted by the maroon corduroy vest and gaucho set Mom recently had made me.

No one at St. Mark Lutheran School—child or adult, boy or girl, mean or kind—bought my act the following day, but I had committed to my lie and played it for all its worth, insisting my ears were, indeed, pierced. I held out for several hours, adamantly refusing to admit I had clapped flimsy ring-tabs onto my ears. Darla and her gang were merciless, and the boys joined in, too. A couple of teachers even had a laugh. One of them told me to remove the pop tabs, but I refused, noting Darla was not being made to remove her earrings. I had known that morning when I walked into my classroom that the jig was up, but I wasn't going to back down. Not when my classmates snorted and hooted, and not when Darla and Terri each grabbed an earlobe and pinched the tabs with all their strength, making my earlobes bleed.

I had one more significant run-in with Darla while we lived in Flint. It was the summer of Nadia Comaneci, and the railroad ties bordering the driveway flower garden made the perfect balance beam. There I was, minding my own business and practicing my dismount when Darla and Terri appeared. I readied myself for teasing but, instead, they took turns slapping me in the face—soft enough not to hurt but hard enough to humiliate. I stood there and took it. Two minutes of happiness flies by, but two minutes of degradation lasts forever. I wish I could say this was the only time Darla had hit me. The other instance was a year earlier when we had been singing along to America's "A Horse with No Name" and disagreed on the meaning of the lyrics. Darla fumed when I didn't acquiesce to her interpretation, so she smacked me. I'd like to go back in time and slap myself for not standing up to her. I didn't tell my parents about either incident until years later, and my mom was dismayed because I hadn't hauled off and hit back at my tormentors.

"Gee, Mom, maybe it was all the 'turn the other cheek' lessons you drilled into me when I was growing up."

"Your father would have loved it if you had punched Darla Nagy in the face."

Damn straight he would have. But adult me knows what kid me did not.

My husband and I have always instructed our son that he shouldn't start a fight, but if somebody brings one to him, he has our unequivocal permission to fight back. My son was offended on my behalf when I told him about the bullying I endured in Flint. He asked if Darla had ever apologized. I told him she had not. He asked if I had forgiven her, and I said that I had, even though it took a few years. Hearing through the proverbial grapevine that

Darla's life has been rough where mine has been smooth, the hurt little girl in me would love to spike the ball and do an end zone dance. But that's not how the Christian life works.

Forgiveness isn't easy, and loving your enemies is a tall order. Praying for those who persecute you—who wants to do that? Left to my own devices, certainly not me. So, I'm thankful I had parents who didn't care about coming out ahead of anybody or having as many material possessions as everyone else. They knew a life built on Christ is the real treasure that gives us our worth. They were human beings who, like every parent and every Christian, screwed things up on occasion, but both of them taught me what victory is all about—eternity spent with my Savior. Considering that, I'm pulling for Darla to win, too.

Chapter Thirteen

New Girl... Again

Holy Trinity Lutheran Church,
Grandview, Missouri, c. 1992

"I'd like for everyone to state their name, then tell the class what his or her father does for a living, and add if you want to follow in his footsteps. Then please explain why or why not."

It was the first hour of the first day of my sophomore year of high school. My English composition teacher, Mrs. Dunnington, thought this was a brilliant method for her class to get to know each other, but I had no intention of playing along. I didn't want to pigeonhole myself as the pastor's kid; furthermore, the LCMS doesn't ordain women. There was no way I was going to get into *that* topic, so when it was my turn, I declined to answer. Mrs. Dunnington was surprised I didn't participate, but my mom was indignant when I told her later that day about the ice breaker. When was I going to learn that too much transparency had its consequences?

"What do you mean you didn't answer the question?" she demanded. "Your teacher and classmates probably think your father is an inmate in the state penitentiary!"

That's the first thing *I* think of when somebody likes their privacy—that they *must* be hiding a felony conviction. In truth, I wasn't ashamed of my dad—far from it. But I wanted one transition to be free of church and anything to do with it.

Fifteen months earlier, I barely said a word to my mother as she steered our Ford LTD southwesterly toward Chicago and St. Louis and, finally, to Kansas City. Dad was driving our brown Ford Granada, which, with its "three on the tree" manual transmission, Mom had tried but failed to master. I hadn't said much to either of my parents for weeks—ever since Dad officially accepted a call to Holy Trinity Lutheran Church in Grandview, Missouri.

Soon after that last bullying incident with Darla in Flint, I became aware we wouldn't remain in Michigan much longer. Mom desired to be closer to extended family, and Dad wanted a different vocational challenge, so he asked the Michigan District to put his name on a call list. Despite cruel treatment from some of my peers, I didn't want to move. I told my parents I loved Flint, but the truth was I didn't want to deal with making friends at yet another church and school. The devil you know and all that. My parents were looking out for my future, too, but I didn't understand that at the time.

Calls started rolling in as soon as vacant congregations became aware my dad was up for grabs. Some were "feelers" from churches wanting to know if he would even entertain the possibility of moving to their town or city. Anything east of the Mississippi River was out, and my mom balked at any place with dreary weather. My parents were taking their time with the decision—this likely would be their last move, and they wanted it to be right. Dad received calls every few weeks, and he strongly considered a few before declining them. Santa Rosa, California, was vetoed because it was, like Flint, too far from relatives. Mapleton and Waverly, Iowa, were strong contenders but ultimately ruled out because none of us wanted to live in a small town.

I was breathing easily until the phone rang one Sunday evening in March. I knew from my dad's demeanor that it was another congregation and that this one might be serious. Dad hung up and said the call was to a church in suburban Kansas City. (The confusion between a Divine Call and a telephone call is made worse by discussing a phone call about a Divine Call. Native Lutheran speakers, especially uber-fluent pastors and their families, inherently understand the difference, but people like my formerly Baptist husband are like, "What the heck?") The call documents from Holy Trinity were due to arrive a few days later, and, unless they contained serious red flags, we would go check out the congregation. Mom didn't want any surprises this time. As it turned out, the call documents and visit were merely a prelude to the inevitable. My parents wanted to get back to the Midwest, and I knew it was a done deal.

My parents and I made the expeditionary visit to Grandview about ten days after Dad received the documents. Brent was by now in his twenties, married, and living in Cleveland, Ohio. It was gray and chilly when we left Flint but warm and sunny when we reached south Kansas City. A local pastor met us in the parking lot at Holy Trinity and escorted us inside the building. I was determined to dislike everything about the place. The outside of the church structure looked weird with its contemporary, triangular, shake-shingled steeple. The inside seemed okay, but the sanctuary was round with three aisles instead of the traditional and wedding-friendly one. The pale linoleum tile floors weren't too attractive, either. Pastor Mehl, our guide, and my dad exchanged enthusiastic conversation about how much easier it is to preach in the round versus to two long columns of people.

Next, we walked one hundred feet to the parsonage, which recently had been converted from a classroom building. The house was considerably less homey than the parsonages we had lived in up to that point, clearly having been constructed to hold students rather than families, but it had in its favor air-conditioning and a dishwasher. Mom wasn't too thrilled with the mottled black, brown, and beige shag carpet in the combination living/dining room, which a sympathetic woman from the congregation accurately pointed out resembled a dead dog. There was plenty of room on the seven-acre church property where Dad could plant a huge garden, and I knew he was thinking about how many tomatoes he could harvest during the hot Missouri summers.

As Pastor Mehl excused himself to make hospital visits, he leaned to whisper in my ear, "Convince your parents to make the move."

His statement surprised me. *I* was the one who needed convincing, and that was not going to happen. I realize now that Pastor Mehl couldn't fail to see my bad attitude and was giving me a pep talk. It didn't work, but, in retrospect, I appreciate his attempt to involve me in the proceedings.

That evening, we attended a congregational forum during which my parents could ask questions ranging from "What style of worship do you prefer?" to "Where is the nearest grocery store?" (The answer to the latter question was "next to the Baptist Church on Main Street." My mom shopped there once, never returning after she received a lecture from the store manager on the evils of drinking when she asked him for the location of the liquor aisle.)

Holy Trinity had been without a pastor for over a year, so the members present were thrilled that my dad was seriously considering their call. My parents were all smiles because there weren't any alarm bells going off in their heads. I didn't notice too many kids my age in attendance. One girl, who introduced herself as Amy Cox, asked if I wanted to sit with her during the meeting. She was a few years older than I and went out of her way to be welcoming, putting me at ease.

On the drive back to Flint, my parents delivered the bad news.

"Sam," my dad began, using his nickname for me, "after praying about it, we believe Grandview is the place God wants us to be." He was uncharacteristically hesitant and clearly heartbroken for me.

"Yeah, I figured," I said, turning to look out the window at the Illinois cornfields so my parents wouldn't see me cry. I imagined them to be indifferent to my feelings, but on a couple of occasions I've caused my own child to do the "look out the window to hide the tears" move, and I know with certainty that it is a knife to a parent's heart.

※

The next four weeks were a flurry of completing the school year, putting the ten acres of land up for sale, Dad wrapping up his duties, Mom packing our belongings (Holy Trinity would have paid for the movers to pack our things, but Donna trusted no one but herself to do an adequate job), and accepting dinner and lunch invitations from dozens of sad members at St. Mark.

On a cool May morning, we pulled out of the driveway on Daly Boulevard for the last time. Dad drove the brown Granada, which towed the Apache camper, and I rode with Mom in the LTD, crowded by a dozen houseplants and miscellaneous breakables. We stopped in Springfield, Illinois, that night, and I sullenly ate my dinner. My parents didn't try to cajole me into a good mood. The next afternoon we rolled into Grandview, and a representative from the van line called to say it would be three more days before our belongings arrived, so Leo and Shirley Schlesselmann invited us to stay at their home.

Lutheran Church-Missouri Synod membership was just over 2.6 million when we moved to Grandview. That sounds like a lot of people, but in many ways the LCMS can be a small world. For example, Mr. Schlesselmann's sister LaVerne was a member at St. Stephen in Liberty, and her son Kenny had been in my Sunday school class there. Mr. Schlesselmann was proud that Holy Trinity had bequeathed its old pews to St. Stephen, which during our tenure had made do with metal folding chairs.

The closely knit nature of our denomination was extra clear on vacations when my parents always found a Missouri Synod church to attend. Without fail, someone always knew, or knew of, my dad at every congregation we visited from New England to New Mexico. On a dozen occasions, people invited us home with them for Sunday dinner. Once, after church in Waynesboro, Virginia, we were treated to a four-course meal served on fine china and crystal in an empty-nester couple's stately dining room. The two hours of conversation and company were so congenial that even I enjoyed the time, and it beat going back to the campground for a lunch of Hamburger Helper.

Years later, when my husband and I decided to vacation in Australia, we invited my parents to come along. The four of us attended a Wednesday Lenten service in tiny Tanunda, South Australia. This, at last, was a place where no one would have any connection to my dad! Speaking afterward to a group of people who were surprised and pleased to have Yank Lutherans in their midst, one woman mentioned that her nephew, Peter Oestmann, studied a few years prior at Concordia Seminary in St. Louis. She asked if my dad had ever met him.

Dad smiled. "I performed his wedding ceremony," he replied. Of course he did.

So, because of the small world of the LCMS, it was old home week at the Schlesselmann house. They conversed easily, and Mrs. Schlesselmann cooked delicious meals, which prompted Mom to solicit the recipe for every coffee cake and casserole we consumed. Between meals, Mom and I went to the parsonage and put away the things we had brought with us in our cars. Dad was already keeping office hours and preparing for his installation. He loved his large, bright workspace with its expanse of bookshelves. Mary, the church secretary, had a hilarious dry wit and was friendlier than the secretary had been at St. Mark. Dad really lucked out with secretaries at Holy Trinity. Mary retired a decade later, and her replacement, Karen, might be the purest of heart person I've ever known. Dad regarded her as a second daughter. Karen and her husband are a decade older than I but always look like they just returned from sessions at a day spa for teenagers.

I don't remember anything about Dad's installation service, probably because at that point I was still determined to leave Kansas City as soon as I was legally able, so there was no need to commit anything to memory at Holy Trinity. A girl named Angie Taylor showed up at the parsonage the following day. She said her grandmother, Helen, had urged her to come and get me outside for a bit. Okay, I did remember meeting Helen at the installation—her smoker's voice was unforgettable. Angie, who with her driver's license and macramé purse was far worldlier and more sophisticated than I, sat on our green floral couch and asked my mom if I could ride with her to Truman Corners, the local shopping center. A few evenings later, Laura Mars joined us for another outing. While we were in Jerry's Sport Shop, someone slapped a Top 40 radio station sticker on the bumper of Angie's car. She and Laura were appalled—they listened to KY-102, the edgier station in town. I decided not to tell them that I listened faithfully to *American Top 40*.

A week later, my parents and I went to a picnic at Laura's grandfather's house. Her parents, siblings, and other relatives were there, too. All the kids ended up in the basement talking about music. Laura and her older brother were arguing about which of Santana's songs was the best—"Oye Como Va" or "Black Magic Woman." I, who a few days earlier had tacked Andy Gibb posters to my bedroom walls, was out of my depth. Other teenagers wore trendy clothing and were pop-culturally aware, but I was the antithesis of cool. I thought it was *Leonard* Skynyrd, for goodness sake. And, unlike me, most of the girls my age didn't need to lose a couple of dozen pounds.

The scale had been my enemy for much of my young life. My first battle with weight occurred when I was ten years old. During a health lesson at St. Mark, the teacher decided to measure each kid's height and weight. Publicly. I was, at that time, five feet five inches, taller than anyone in the class, and embarrassingly curvy. When I tipped the scale at 110 pounds, everyone laughed. I was mortified. I wasn't overweight, but everyone treated me as though I was, so why not have an extra helping of potatoes at dinner? By the time we moved to Grandview, I was legitimately too heavy. This became clear to me on the congregational camping trip a month later.

Most of the youth group was swimming in the lake when I arrived with my parents. I didn't bring along a swimsuit, primarily because I don't like lake water. The Johnsons were taking out their boat and invited me along. Being *on* the water sounded like fun, so I jumped at the chance to avoid uncomfortable conversation with my peer group. While hopping from shore onto the boat's deck, I slipped and fell into the water. Well played, Irony. Amy Cox, who again was kindness personified, fished me out and said I could borrow one of her outfits. Her shirt fit me, but the shorts wouldn't zip, so Barbara Lute offered me a pair of cut-offs. My heart sank. Barbara was a nice girl, but I was certain she outweighed me by a good thirty pounds. Her shorts fit me perfectly. I immediately resolved to lose weight before starting a new school in the fall.

Fourteen-year-olds take for granted their healthy knees and the ability to drop pounds quickly, and I was no exception. All it took was mowing the lawn once a week and refusing dessert, and the weight melted away. My parents took me to the mall, but my fashion sense was zero. I selected some clothes that were more appropriate for a middle-aged woman in an office typing pool than a girl going into ninth grade.

I was lamb dressed as mutton when I boarded the bus to Grandview West Junior High. Every other kid at Holy Trinity attended East Junior High, but the parsonage was right over the school boundary line, so I was headed to a school where I didn't know anyone. I wore new white slacks with a blue blouse and sling-back heels.

The day was a mixed bag. First hour was home economics, and I liked my tablemates, three of whom were also named Karen, and the teacher, who was missing two fingers at the second knuckle. Rumor had it she accidentally chopped them off one day during class, and they had ended up in a pasta dish. To my surprise, I enjoyed my biology and algebra classes and teachers. I didn't care for gym, English, or typing. The typing teacher was a sour, intimidating woman. I had never used an electric typewriter, and when I raised my hand to ask a rudimentary question, she made fun of it, eliciting laughter from my peers. Later, on my way off the bus, I tripped and sprawled on the ground, ripping my polyester pants. My parents, waiting at the parsonage door, hungry for news that I'd had a good day, looked anguished as I rushed past them to my room where I could cry in peace.

I made acquaintances rather than friends at school that year and concentrated on doing well in my classes. Although I still didn't love Grandview, my resentment was fading. I started Grandview High School the following year, joined Foreign Language Club and Library Club, and participated in extemporaneous speaking competitions. Somehow, despite my efforts to hide it, teachers and kids found out my dad was a pastor, and it didn't seem to matter.

I was featured in the yearbook for my nerdy pen pal hobby. Shortly after we moved to Grandview, I decided I wanted a foreign pen pal like my mom had when she was a teenager. She and her correspondence partner, June, from Manchester in the United Kingdom, began writing each other shortly after the end of World War II. I thought that sounded like fun, so I answered a magazine ad for foreign teenagers seeking American pen pals. The response was overwhelming. I received no fewer than two hundred letters from a dozen European countries and Australia. There was only one inappropriate letter, a request from a thirty-year-old Norwegian man who wanted more than the occasional note. I picked the ten most intriguing letters and began writing. I looked ridiculous in the yearbook photos, dressed in the wrap skirt I had sewn in ninth grade home ec, with my untamed curly hair, and wearing those sling-backs that would have looked better on a woman five times my age. I made some strange sartorial choices in high school. There was my perimenopausal lady look, my preppy phase, and the unfortunate colorful baggy pants paired with stiletto heels trend. Sometimes I looked like June Cleaver, a Kennedy, and a hooker all in one week.

Like most teenagers, I had yet to figure out my place in life. Between the adjustment to new people and an unfamiliar church culture, I lost myself, and I wanted to create a version of me that would give me a chance at either fitting in when it suited me or going unnoticed when it didn't. I was tired of every few years being the new girl who had to plug in to a pre-existing situation, of trying to make friends. It didn't help that I felt years older than my peers. My mom's efforts to produce the perfectly behaved child created a teenager who was unable to act her age.

"I went into the sanctuary at church every day and prayed for you when you were in school," Dad told me years later.

His prayers bore fruit because, at some point during high school, I acquired a healthy amount of self-esteem. Although I would have been loath to admit it at the time, meeting people and navigating alien places gave me a backbone. I didn't like *how* my spine came to grow so sturdy, but now I appreciate its strength. My parents sympathized and, more importantly, prayed for me during my time of adjustment. They let me be me through strange clothing choices and haircuts, and they never told me to adjust my attitude as I was acclimating to my environment.

Instead, they trusted God to do His work of walking with me on good days and bad.

❦

At church, I enjoyed the youth group and was elected its president during my junior year of high school. I don't remember spearheading anything significant, except scheduling a bake sale or two. Laura Mars and I spent considerable time planning La Rize, a seven-story bar and dance venue that, when built, would feature a different music style on each floor: country, disco, classic rock, new wave, punk, pop, and blues. Every Sunday after church, we met in the narthex to sketch crude building elevations and ponder which music style should be showcased on the seventh floor. We were confident we would make our fortunes on this enterprise, although we had no notion of financing, permits, or marketing. I didn't even know what property tax was.

Our plans for La Rize halted when Laura and I left for separate colleges, but not before Mark Heard and Lee Ann Cox, who were in their twenties, came to one of our evening youth events, a disco in the church basement, and taught us their best *Saturday Night Fever* dance moves. Some of us tried to copy them but ended up doing the Electric Slide and the Bus Stop while the Kroll sisters, dressed like Old Order Mennonites, waltzed with each other in the corner.

June and Rebecca, with their long dresses and old-fashioned manners, were often the subject of snide talk, including my own. I'm ashamed of myself now. Who was I to talk and make fun with my sling-back heels and shirtwaist dresses? I had no business judging anyone for their clothing and should have kept my mouth shut, even more so because I had been bullied in prior years. Far more significantly, I was a Christian and not acting like one. The Kroll girls' IQs might have totaled more than the rest of the youth group put together. They were serious and gracious young women, and they lived their faith by treating everyone they encountered with dignity. I should have emulated them, rather than participating in their mockery. If I ever doubt my need for salvation, I only have to look at some of the ways I've chosen to behave for proof that I, in the words of John Newton, am a great sinner, making me eternally thankful that Christ is a great Savior.

After high school, I started college with no idea what I wanted to do with my life. Everybody, it seemed, was majoring in business in the 1980s, so I assumed I should, too. My gifts were in foreign language and communication, but I decided to go with an area of study that requires an understanding of numbers.

"Economics," I told the registrar when he asked for my intended major during class enrollment at Northwest Missouri State University. My dad, standing nearby, had to be thinking, "Are you kidding me? This girl can't do math above algebra without crying." But he remained quiet and let me do my thing—which included failing Economics 101 my first semester before switching to an English literature major and political science minor.

The summer before I left for college, my parents purchased their own home and moved nine miles south to Raymore, Missouri. Because the Holy Trinity parsonage was easily accessed via sidewalk from the church, foot traffic was high at any time of day. In Raymore, Mom and Dad could drink their morning coffee, eat their meals, and watch *Dallas* without interruption. And they could paint the walls whatever color they desired.

Because I only spent summers and school breaks there, this house, like the parsonages before it, initially didn't seem like home. It felt at the time like a kind of limbo for me. I'm one of those people who misses out on a lot because I'm always looking ahead to the next thing to enjoy, the next thing to worry about. Living in the moment has never been my forte. My parents' house didn't feel like home to me until I had my own place, my own bills, my own spouse, and my own dinners to cook. Then I longed to sit at their table, eating my mom's pot roast and the vegetables my dad grew in his garden. There is no more beautiful noise than the sounds made by people you love: my dad putting the coffee pot back in its place after pouring a late afternoon cup, or my mom pulling pots and pans out to make dinner. I miss my parents' clangs and rustles, their tangible, everyday hum that, I finally understand, made walls and floors into a home.

I was a member of HT (Dad and I affectionately abbreviated the name in conversation) only until I married, and I didn't feel all that connected to the place during my membership time. It, too, felt like a place marker until I could pick my own church. But the congregation's importance to me has grown. I have over time, via book clubs, fundraisers, and fellowship dinners, often been more involved at Holy Trinity than at my own places of worship. When Jim and I sent our son to preschool, Holy Trinity was our first and only choice.

Every congregation has a unique culture and personality, and every member takes away something unique from his or her relationship with it. In my case, Holy Trinity and its people have, in the words of Psalm 90:12, taught me to number my days. When we arrived in Grandview, I was a teenager, and now I'm the parent of one. My parents were younger when Dad began his ministry there than I am now. Some people with whom I was in the youth group are grandparents. Laura Mars and I were *just* sneaking out of a youth retreat to play tennis, racing down a stairwell away from our youth leader. Now Laura is a leader, and a good one. Jimmy Peacock was, mere months ago it seems, the organist's little boy. Now he's grown-up Jim and is the president of the congregation. None of this took long at all.

While I am not an official member of this church family, which thrives despite societal changes and challenges, I am blessed to be a peripheral part of it. Holy Trinity is not the sum of its physical components: the white linoleum floors that cause too much glare in wedding photos, the short aisle that makes for a brief bridal processional, and the architecture that channels the 1970s. No, the marrow of Holy Trinity is the people who work tirelessly to make something exceptional out of Vacation Bible School, youth events, staff retirements, and things as commonplace as potluck dinners.

With every table that they set up, every pan of red cabbage they cook, every school supply or canned good they collect for children in their community, the people of HT pen a love letter to their church home and family.

My dad ended his active pastoral ministry at Holy Trinity when he retired in 1996. He was named pastor emeritus shortly after and never lacked the opportunity to preach or lead Bible studies, but his days of weekly sermons and ministering were over. He knew it was time to "change gears," as he put it, but he was sad to leave, full-time, the calling he loved. My brother and I were asked to say a few words at the retirement dinner the congregation hosted for my parents. Brent stood and spoke beautifully about how our dad was an example of faith and a person of diligent prayer.

Several hundred people were in attendance and, when it came time for me to speak, I wanted to make redress for what I had once left unsaid. I told about the incident in high school composition class when the teacher asked each student to introduce themselves and say what his or her father did for a living.

"I was too embarrassed to say this when I was fifteen years old, but now I say it with pride," I told the crowd. "My name is Karen Kuhlmann, my father is a Lutheran Church-Missouri Synod pastor, and I could never follow in his footsteps or fill his shoes."

The noise of my parents' daily routines conveyed "home" to me, and so have the sounds of church: the choir director's staccato footsteps across the tile floors; spoons banging against the sides of casserole dishes during potluck dinners; side-splitting laughter during a preschool auction fundraiser; "Merry Christmas!" said over and over after the Christmas Eve candlelight service, people staying to chat longer than usual because kids are home from college and no one wants the holiday high to end. And soft voices in the narthex as people file by the photo display of someone who was alive at church on Sunday but asleep in Christ on Thursday.

My mother-in-law once asked me if my family had a lot of reunions.

"We do," I answered. "We call them funerals." Shortly after my husband and I were married, we went to a wedding every few weeks; now, it feels like we go to funerals at the same rate.

I have fond memories of many people from both Liberty and Flint, but I was never part of the extended life cycles of those congregations. At Holy Trinity, I've witnessed young people grow old, and old people die. Too many young people have died, too.

I grew up among the people of Holy Trinity and will, though not a member there but among them still, grow as old as God wants me to be. Through the gift of knowing the people at HT, God is teaching me to number my days. Now, if I can gain a heart of wisdom in the process, I'll be complete.

Chapter Fourteen

Shopping Spree

My parents, me, Jim, and Jim's
parents, 1992
(When Jim still thought he wouldn't
be a Lutheran)

It was important to my parents that I marry well, and they didn't mean marrying someone with a good job. Marrying well meant, to my dad, someone who loved Christ and who put that love into practice. And who had a job. To my mom, it meant finding a Missouri Synod Lutheran, period.

Mom could really pontificate on the subject, too. I dreaded the resulting lecture if a relative divorced after marrying outside the denomination. Mom refused to attribute the divorce to anything but the "mixed marriage."

"That's why *you* will marry a Lutheran, Karen Ann," she insisted. Missouri Synod is implied here. A Wisconsin Synod Lutheran or, worse, a member of the more liberal Evangelical Lutheran Church in America was as undesirable to Mom as a Pentecostal, Scientologist, or Zoroastrian.

Although my dad didn't browbeat me, he reminded me of the importance of candid discussion regarding faith and church attendance before committing to an engagement. I listened to and heeded his advice until I started dating the man I would marry—a Baptist who attended a Presbyterian church.

Jim grew up in the American Baptist denomination. Just as no two Lutheran bodies are completely alike, American Baptists differ from, say, Old Regular Baptists, Landmark Baptists, and Southern Baptists—the latter of which Jim's mom adhered to from her childhood. If I had known when I started dating Jim that Millie liked to claim "Hard Shell Baptist" status, which Merriam-Webster defines as "a strict and uncompromising Baptist,"[1] I may not have gone out with him in the first place.

Jim and I were set up by a mutual friend. I worked with Kevan, and Jim hung out with him at a Kansas City Presbyterian church famous for its singles' group. Kevan was also Baptist, but he cautioned me that my date might be more representative of Baptist social mores than was he. Kevan was an ardent proponent of Believer's baptism (not infants) and eternal security (once saved, always saved), but if he had ever sworn to avoid alcohol, he was breaking his vow. During our weekly office outing for Mexican food, Kevan was the first to suggest margaritas—two pitchers for five people. At lunchtime.

The night of my blind date with Jim arrived. He picked me up, and we started the evening at Olive Garden, where I ordered wine, thinking that if he balked about me drinking it and him paying for it, then we weren't meant to be. A legalism litmus test, if you will. Fortunately, it turned out Jim was a lapsed Baptist, one who had years ago gone on a Hawaiian drinking cruise with his Mennonite college buddies. One glass of house Chardonnay was not going to scare him off.

A few dates later, we still had not talked about our respective beliefs—something that, had my parents known, would have caused them acute disappointment. I remained silent on the subject out of fear that Jim was commitment-phobic and would construe any such discussion as an attempt on my part to figure out where we would have our wedding. I later learned he was reluctant to broach the topic because he was unfamiliar with Lutheranism in general, and the extra Missouri Synod tag made him worry his new girlfriend was part of a weird, cultic subset. We were dining at a restaurant on Kansas City's Country Club Plaza, eating chips and salsa, drinking beer, and watching a male exotic dancer entertain a bridal shower party at the next table when Jim picked his moment to ask, "So, how do you believe you are saved?"

A Lutheran would probably never use that phrase. We might ask someone, "How do you believe you go to Heaven?" or, more realistically, we avoid the question altogether and hope to someday bump into the person on the streets of Paradise. No sense making either party uncomfortable in the meantime.

But Jim had asked the question, and I hoped my answer was satisfactory. I was certain we believed the same thing about salvation.

"I believe Christ died to save me from my sins, and that's why I believe I'll be in Heaven for eternity." I felt awkward saying this with a stripper a few feet away. I also was annoyed that *I* was the one being put on the spot to defend my beliefs. Jim was clearly trying to ascertain if I believed in salvation by grace through faith. I mean, Hello? The Reformation? Martin Luther? I tried to ignore my parents' voices in my head—the ones that were telling me I should be as proactive as my boyfriend on this subject.

Our conversation was shorter than the stripper's routine, but at least the subject was in play. Jim even invited me to go with him to the Bible study he regularly attended at Colonial Presbyterian—one of the city's largest churches and home of the renowned singles' group. I began accompanying him to this class where I met a lot of terrifically nice people who talked with sincerity about what God was doing in their lives. Over several months of dating, we enjoyed golf tournaments, softball games, and brunches with this group. We also made regular trips to sports bars for Kansas City Chiefs football and beer. The people from Colonial were tremendous, but I knew Presbyterianism and I were not made for each other.

I still went to Holy Trinity for church, but I didn't invite Jim since meeting my pastor meant meeting my dad, and I was waiting to meet his parents before introducing him to mine. About three months into our relationship, we had a dating milestone. Jim wanted me to meet some hometown friends from Hutchinson, Kansas, who were in our area for the weekend. I drove to his apartment on a Saturday evening, eager to make a good impression.

Tim and Becky struck me immediately as committed and sincere Christians, but meeting them was like being introduced to members of an alien race. Devout Mennonite aliens. They were, specifically, Mennonite Brethren. Jim, Tim, and Tim's brother, Rick, had all graduated from Tabor College, a tiny Mennonite Brethren-affiliated school in Hillsboro, Kansas. Jim told me Rick and some friends of his had nearly been expelled from Tabor for stealing an American flag from an area business and running it up the flagpole on Tabor's campus. Mennonites of every stripe hold the doctrine of pacifism and nonviolence. They also avoid displays of nationalism; hence, most Mennonite institutions do not display the flag. Lutherans, conversely, display both Christian and American flags in our sanctuaries.

After Jim introduced me to Tim and Becky, they at once started talking about their lives in Christ. They questioned me about mine, too, although it took me awhile to figure that out.

"So, Karen," Tim began, "do you like Carman?"

"The opera?" I had not pegged these two as Bizet fans.

"No, the contemporary Christian singer," Tim explained.

"I'm not really familiar with her," I admitted.

"Carman is a man."

"Oh." Cue the uncomfortable silence.

"So, Karen," Tim now ventured, "how do you spend your quiet time?"

I had heard Jim use this phrase before. I figured it was central Kansas vernacular for free time.

"I watch TV or go shopping," I answered. "I like to ride my bike, too."

"No, Karen," Tim said. "Your *quiet time.*"

"Well, I guess if I'm really in need of peace and quiet, I read."

"What are you reading right now for your quiet time?" Tim persisted.

Okay, what was *with* these people, and why was it so important for them to know what I did in my spare time?

"I'm not reading anything right now, but I like a good thriller," I explained.

More uncomfortable silence. They either didn't like spy novels or I had, again, misunderstood the line of inquiry.

Tim sighed, clearly disappointed in me. "What are you reading to draw closer to the Lord?"

Oh. Quiet time meant *devotions*. Why didn't he say so in the first place? I quickly made up something.

"Well, I was reading a passage in Galatians the other day. It was about the attributes a Christian should display like love and joy and—" Becky cut me off before I could finish.

"It's Galatians five, verses twenty-two and twenty-three, Karen, and it talks about the fruits of the Spirit." She dismissed me and reminded Jim her favorite television show, *The Young Riders*, was about to start; with that, I was off the hook. I was by this time, however, feeling zero love, joy, peace, patience, kindness, goodness, faithfulness, or gentleness, but managed to summon a shred of self-control as we sat to watch the wholesome dramatization of the Pony Express. I wished I were dating a Lutheran.

All during the show, which featured an abundance of double-barreled shotguns and Colt and Remington pistols, weapons suggestive of non-pacifism, Tim and Becky cuddled and giggled on the couch while Jim and I sat in chairs across the room from each other.

"We're married, so we can do this," Becky taunted. "You two have to be good."

It made me want to drop down on the floor with Jim and go at it like rabbits just to piss her off.

When, a few weeks later, Jim invited me to meet his family, I worried they'd be Tim and Becky 2.0. Jim's parents were going to be in nearby Lawrence, Kansas, visiting his sister, and he wanted me to have dinner with them. I was glad to meet them finally but afraid I would make as bad an impression on Jim's family as I had on his friends.

"Hi, Mrs. Averitt," I greeted Jim's mother in the kitchen. "It's really nice to meet you."

Millie looked up from the sink where she was working. "Jim *loves* strawberries," she said and went back to making dinner.

That non sequitur out of the way, we had a great evening. Jim's parents, both nervous Southerners, desired to make people comfortable and well-fed. The only awkward moment for me was when we prayed before dinner. I had seen a Baptist family (the Waltons on TV) hold hands when they prayed but had never done so myself. I was uncomfortable with it then, and I still don't care for the practice. Lutherans tend to keep our hands to ourselves when we pray. Whenever Jim and I host his family for Thanksgiving or Easter, he rushes to instruct everyone to fold hands before his sister can engineer a tactile circle of togetherness.

Not long after that first meeting with his family, I took Jim home to meet my parents. I remember little about the evening except that Mom and Dad clearly adored my boyfriend and that everyone was comfortable with each other. Jim was thrilled when my dad offered him a Milwaukee's Best beer from a twelve-pack he had purchased for $3.99. It was one of those occasions when I was proud of everybody in the room. There was an immediate rapport and affection between Jim and my parents that from that evening never waned.

Five months later, Jim proposed. I'm ashamed to admit we still hadn't talked about where we would go to church if things became serious. They were serious now, and I knew I didn't want to switch denominations. I was hoping Jim would roll over, play dead, and do things my way. My mom kept asking if Jim was going to take Lutheran instruction classes. She reminded me what would happen if we raised children outside of the LCMS.

"You know what I'll do, Karen Ann," she warned. "I will baptize them in the bathtub." Once more for emphasis. "I will *baptize* them in the bathtub!"

Meanwhile, Jim's mom, thinking she was brokering a compromise, said her cousin in South Carolina had informed her that the Methodists would welcome us with open arms.

Our respective parents didn't meet each other until eight weeks before our wedding. We gathered at the house we had recently purchased. Jim was already living there, and I would move in after the wedding. Jim's parents, sister, and her family arrived first. I was uneasy. I knew my parents would like the Averitts, but I wasn't sure the feeling would be mutual.

To the world at large, Missouri Synod Lutherans are uptight, conservative, and reserved. We feel that way about ourselves sometimes. We don't, however, have legalistic views on alcohol, tobacco, movie-going, card-playing, or dancing. When Jim was growing up, his congregation recited in unison a creed in which one pledged to "avoid strong drink." One drink meant you were not living for Christ. Two meant you might be an alcoholic. Three probably meant you were destined for the third circle of Hell. As I've mentioned, my dad enjoyed a beer or two after mowing, and my mom claimed that "nothing tastes better than a beer after cleaning the house." Jim's parents might as well have been meeting Keith Richards and Courtney Love.

My dad, still a smoker at that time, held it together for four hours during the visit. A good thing, too, because Jim's dad talked at length about one of his favorite hobbies—square dancing. Square dancing was, according to Bill, the one acceptable form of dance because of its wholesomeness.

"Square dancers don't drink or smoke," he boasted while my dad sat there jonesing for a Camel.

❦

Our house "north of the river" might as well have been in Luxembourg. The Missouri River divides Kansas City into distinct parts, and our new home felt far away from where I had finally put down roots in Grandview, which is landlocked by south Kansas City. My debilitating bridge phobia also made living north a ridiculous choice, but we loved our house, and Jim and I together made the commute downtown to our respective jobs.

Jim and I agreed after our wedding to check out several churches of differing denominations. I knew that only LCMS churches would pass muster with me, but I kept that fact to myself. Holy Trinity was not on the list. The distance, twenty-four miles, was prohibitive, and Jim resisted what he assumed was the expectation of some HT members—that we would join the congregation his father-in-law pastored. I wasn't happy excluding my church from consideration, but I acknowledged my husband's legitimate wish to set some boundaries. Also, it made me look completely on board with the whole "find a church that suits us both" thing.

The first place on our list was an American Baptist church near our house. Unlike the Baptist congregations I had previously visited, I didn't dislike this one on sight. It had stained glass windows, paraments in the proper color for the liturgical year, and no tissues in the pews. I assumed this meant we would not be treated to a dramatic end-of-service altar call where the pastor would stress the need for rescue from sin (being a sinner, I had no problem with that part) before working everyone into an emotional frenzy when shouts of "Amen!" or "That's right, Brother!" would accompany hugs and tears. But everything seemed normal. Surprisingly, it was Jim who needed to keep a lid on the snark.

The pastor, uncharacteristically for Baptists, wore a robe instead of a suit. He looked okay to me, but I noticed Jim was trying to stifle laughter.

"What's so funny?" I mouthed.

"Martin Mull."

"What?"

"He looks like Martin Mull," my husband whispered.

Jim was right. I hadn't seen enough of Martin Mull's film and television work for this to impact me, but Jim was having trouble focusing because of the guy's uncanny resemblance to the actor. I was fine until halfway through the service when the pastor turned his back to the congregation and felt around for something behind the altar. He slipped a strap over his head and whipped around, Johnny Cash-style, to reveal an acoustic guitar. He proceeded to sing a set of 1970s folk songs while we tried our best to look impassive. We had made the classic visitor mistake of sitting too close to the front, and we didn't want to embarrass the pastor or ourselves by laughing. On the drive home, Jim said he hadn't loved the place. I was glad he spoke first so I didn't have to burn a "no" vote of my own.

The next non-LCMS church we visited was in the Evangelical Free denomination. The congregation was newly formed and didn't yet have its own building, so they worshipped in a funeral home chapel. The order of worship was similar to the one in *The Lutheran Hymnal*. The funeral home organ rendered the music a tad mournful, but some Lutheran pastors are guilty of picking some truly horrible dirges because the words complement the Bible readings for the day, so I had no legitimate gripe there. In truth, there was a lot to like about the service. The real revelation about what this church had going for it, though, came afterward. Three couples our age corralled Jim and me, welcoming us to visit again, encouraging us to join the church, and inviting us to brunch.

"Do you have children?" one woman asked.

"No," I replied. "Not yet."

"Do you have plans—" Whoa! We had met mere moments ago, and she was curious about our baby-making timetable.

"—for lunch?" she finished.

Because it was Mother's Day and we were headed to my parents' house for dinner, we didn't accept the invitation. During the drive to their place, I prepared myself for Mom's interrogation about where we had worshipped that morning. I also pondered the friendliness of the people we had met. Their overtures were sincere—I was certain of that. It stood in stark contrast to one of the Missouri Synod churches Jim and I had attended recently where everybody, including the pastor, ignored us. That didn't surprise me. I had been around prickly German Lutherans all my life. Too often, LCMS members don't even speak to people they have known for years—people with whom they kneel week after week at the communion rail. Jim didn't want to jump into an environment like that, and I couldn't blame him. He really liked the Evangelical Free funeral home church, both the denomination and the people we met. I liked the people, too, but the denomination doesn't practice infant baptism, and that was a deal breaker for me.

A few weeks later, Jim suggested we check out a non-denominational service he had heard about from a friend. The group worshipped on Sunday mornings in a bank. (Yes, I rolled my eyes when my husband told me this.) Jim and I were overdressed, me in a skirt and blouse and Jim in khaki pants and a polo shirt, compared to everybody else the day we visited.

The pre-service music started a few minutes after we arrived. Seven songs in, I was tired of praising. Each song had a chorus longer than the last. After singing the lone line, "He is worthy," twenty times, I'd had enough. Okay, we get the point—stop already with the hands raised to the ceiling, and the closed eyes and the swaying!

There were two more songs, the praise leader told us. Everyone was invited to share their talents. The woman in front of us moved the jacket on the chair next to her to reveal a tambourine. She turned to speak to us.

"The Lord gave me this tambourine."

"That's not fair," Jim whispered to me. "He didn't give us one."

After enduring all the talent in the room, the pastor, or some guy who happened to be speaking that day, gave a talk about financial planning. At no time did I hear about my need for a savior or who that Savior is. I did hear about Charles Schwab and his plan for saving my financial future. There was also a recommendation for a certain brand of vacuum cleaner.

Finally, it was time to go (Thank you, Jesus!), but first, there was a treat in store. A husband and wife were going to perform some special music. *What?* There is only so much music one can take in a single church service.

The duo assumed their places up front, each dressed in a black turtleneck and black slacks. She had straight black hair down to her waist, which moved as she sang and swayed. Her husband strummed an acoustic guitar and hummed along, one finger occasionally darting to the bridge of his wire-frame glasses. We were free to leave once John and Yoko's clones finished their set.

I could have sworn the service had lasted three hours, but it had been only ninety minutes. All Jim said was, "Oh, man," and I knew the LCMS was looking better and better to him.

❦

As strange as some of these services were, I will admit to cringing when the uninitiated visit a Missouri Synod congregation. I'm not ashamed of the theology they will hear. No, it's the liturgy, our gorgeous, straight-from-the-Bible, Latin-labled, confusing liturgy that makes me wince when my mother-in-law visits a typical service and she can't figure out her Nunc Dimittus from her Agnus Dei. The Te Deum Laudemas and the Venite? Let's not even go there. Millie has faithfully attended worship for more than eighty years, so even though she isn't comfortable in a Lutheran setting, she knows what church is about. What happens to the family who wanders in one Sunday, never having been to church, and the order of service makes zero sense to them? What if they sit next to me? Do I assist them by pointing out the various components of the liturgy, or would I be more helpful by allowing them some anonymity? For most of my life, I've erred on the side of leaving them to their own devices, convinced I've done them a favor. But have I? It's true that some visitors want to be left alone, but I'm guessing that most people who work up the nerve to check out a church for the first time would welcome some encouragement.

Although the LCMS order of service is imprinted on the DNA of lifers like me, that doesn't mean we can't get tripped up. One part of the liturgy from *The Lutheran Hymnal,* which was used in the LCMS during my childhood, always confounded me. It took place directly before and after the Gospel reading. The pastor (in my case, Dad) announced the reading by saying, for example, "The Holy Gospel is from John chapter three, beginning at the sixteenth verse."

The congregation responded by standing and singing, "Glory be to Thee, O Lord!"[2]

After the reading, the pastor/Dad said, "Here ends the Gospel," after which was sung the phrase, "Praise be to Thee, O Christ."[3]

In childhood, I had difficulty remembering which came first— "Lord" or "Christ"? The names are, after all, easily interchanged. I regularly failed to sing the correct one, so I sought the advice of my teenage brother who, it turned out, had the same problem. Brent gave me a device so useful for recalling the proper order of this part of the liturgy that I never again messed up.

"You know L.C. Greenwood who plays for the Steelers?" Brent asked me. I did. Church wasn't our family's only constant on Sundays.

"I think of his initials right before the Gospel," he said, turning his attention back to the Alice Cooper album cover he was reading. "That's how I remember 'Lord' comes before 'Christ'."

I've used this memory jogger ever since. It probably would have surprised the late, six-time All-Pro defensive lineman that two good Lutheran kids prepared for the Gospel reading every Sunday by chanting to themselves, "L.C. Greenwood, L.C. Greenwood."

❧

During our search for a congregation that would suit both Jim and me, I really did try, up to a point, to see things from his perspective. After investigating a few more LCMS churches, we visited what turned out to be a charismatic service. They did everything but bring out snakes. I'm not at all suggesting these people were not devout Christians. I am, however, completely affirming that no Lutheran I know would have been remotely comfortable with what went on that morning. People were talking about faith healing and speaking in tongues, and I sat there worried they were going to exhibit their gifts. Lutherans believe in spiritual gifts, but, honestly, we're thrilled that we have been passed over for the showier ones.

I was not surprised on this day by the praise songs with repetitive choruses. It was no shock that everyone was dressed in jeans and t-shirts because, as someone on stage explained, "Jesus was a casual guy." As I sat there, I wished I were sitting by someone with the mere gift of a tambourine. Instead, I was surrounded by people supposedly gifted with the ability to prophesy. The pastor asked the group if anyone "had a word." People stood up left and right and in dreamy voices said things like, "God loves everyone here today," and "Someone here will get sick and then get better."

After a half hour of what they termed prophesying, it was time for the message, which centered on the pastor's wife and her gift of driving out evil spirits.

"Our girls know that sometimes when they come home from school, Mommy will be performing an exorcism at the kitchen table," the pastor said. He could not have teed up my moment any better. "I can't do this," I told Jim as we walked to our car after the service. "It's time for you to become a Lutheran."

My husband, who hates weirdness as much as I do, agreed.

My mom was thrilled. Her nightmare scenario of me becoming Presbyterian or Methodist had not materialized. Dad was nonchalant. Although he had zero faith in me regarding things like car maintenance ("You're two quarts low on oil—do you want to burn up your engine?"), he trusted me with the big picture.

Many Lutheran parents worry when their sons or daughters date or become engaged to someone from another denomination. Honestly, I used to think I would be heartbroken if my son chose someday to marry a Baptist or a non-denominational gal. Jim, now a firmly established Missouri Synod Lutheran, has helped me soften my views.

"What if our son marries a Lutheran who doesn't care about her faith and they end up as Christmas and Easter Christians?" he asks. "If you had a choice between that and his marrying a Baptist who is strong in her faith and lives it out every day, which would you pick?"

Knowing full well that Missouri Synod Lutherans do not have a corner on salvation, and that walking with Christ isn't getting any easier in this world, I agree with him. "I'd go with the Baptist."

"Okay," Jim says, happy that I can see reason.

"But I will baptize their children in the bathtub." And, in case he didn't understand me the first time, "I will *baptize* them in the bathtub!"

Chapter Fifteen

All is Calm?

Christmas, Liberty, Missouri, 1966

I hate to admit this, especially to my fellow Christians, but I really don't enjoy Christmas. When I was a child, I was so keyed up in anticipation that I didn't sleep much in December. I'm not sure if the thrill is gone because I'm an adult, or because the celebration of Christmas in suburban America and its churches drains and frustrates me. Maybe it's some of both. A Christian shouldn't feel this way, right? I'm supposed to be peaceful and joyful 24/7 from Thanksgiving through Epiphany. But during Advent, the season of the church year that precedes Christmas, when I should be preparing my heart to celebrate the birth of my Savior, the Prince of Peace, what am I doing instead?

I'm shopping for electronics and for little gifts to have on hand to give people who might give *me* little gifts so there are no hurt feelings if a surprise little gift isn't reciprocated. I'm decorating my house with stuff I don't even like and then have to dust for the next four weeks. I finally understand why my mom used to bribe me to decorate *her* house. In addition to decorating, there is gift wrap and tape to buy, and I have to return to the store because I always forget the tape. When I arrive home, I find three years' worth of tape in our basement. Then it's back to the store to buy more stuff that my family doesn't want or need. After all, it would be a travesty not to have a mountain of presents under the tree, because that is how we show love!

Many Christians do Christmas this way. We who are supposed to be all about the real reason for the season act like everybody else. I get a good laugh from the annual Christian anger at retailers. How dare Target cashiers say "Happy Holidays" instead of "Merry Christmas" when ringing up all that loot? Why do believers rage because Starbucks once removed snowflakes from their seasonal red cups? Did that somehow make Christ's birth less consequential? Corporations that transparently attempt to make a profit (which, as I understand it, is the whole point of selling things) aren't the bad guys here. Too many of us Christians long ago sold out the "Silent Night" version of Christmas with its heavenly peace in favor of the "Silver Bells" edition with its busy sidewalks.

I don't remember Christmas being crazy when I was growing up. Less money meant fewer trips to the mall, presumably. My mom baked a myriad of cookies, and she bought my brother and me several presents each without going overboard. One predictable gift was the embroidery floss and stamped pillowcases that she gave me every year beginning when I was eight years old so that I could improve my needlework skills. It was as though she was preparing me for life in Jane Austen's time.

"Your French knots are sloppy," Mom regularly scolded me.

"I hate embroidery!" I wailed. "Why can't we have normal pillowcases?"

This never went down well. "It's not Christian to complain, young lady."

"I bet Jesus hates embroidery just as much as I do!"

"Marvin, did you *hear* your daughter?" She wanted to pin a blasphemy charge on me, too.

"Yep," my dad replied from behind the sports page. "I don't think Jesus cares much for yarn."

"It's *floss*, Marvin!"

Mom also bought me a doll every Christmas. One year it was Betsy Wetsy, and I discovered when I cut off Betsy's fingers that she "wet" from her hands as well as from the usual spot. Another year, my Baby Alive came with powdered food that I mixed with water and fed to my doll. It smelled bad after a few weeks, so Mom held it under the kitchen faucet and washed the doll's cavity as if it were a Thanksgiving turkey. Then there was my Chrissy doll. Remember her? She had long red hair, an orange lace dress with bell sleeves, and a Quasimodo-like knob on her back. When I turned the knob, her long hair disappeared down the hole in her scalp, resulting in a shorter 'do. A week after my parents gave her to me, I cut off most of Chrissy's hair.

"Karen Ann," Mom chided, "we got you that doll because of her hair!"

I shrugged in response.

"Don't you have anything to say for yourself?"

"How come you never buy me a Lite Brite?" I asked.

"Honestly, Karen Ann!"

"Honestly, *what?*" But I knew what. I had earned my reputation as the child who didn't take care of anything. Whether coloring the interiors of my dresser drawers or holding a sparkler against our new patio lounge chair to see if I could melt plastic, I had proven I couldn't keep anything nice.

"You will have those tiny lights strewn all over the house on day one, and I will not have them ruining my vacuum cleaner!"

I never got a Lite Brite, and Chrissy was the last doll my parents gave me; but even with our mother-daughter skirmishes over my carelessness, the Christmases of my childhood were more worshipful and wondrous than the ones I now celebrate.

❦

My dad enjoyed Christmas more than my mom did—probably because their respective memories of childhood Christmases were radically different. The Kuhlmann celebration in Nebraska began with the Christmas Eve church service, after which dozens of aunts, uncles, and cousins came to my grandparents' house to eat a late dinner and open presents. Still clutching the bags of hard candy and oranges the ushers had given them at church, the kids ran to the parlor where they marveled at the giant fire hazard that a couple of uncles had stayed back to assemble. Mercury glass decorations and scores of clip-on candles adorned the tree. My adult dad and Uncle Dale used to roar with laughter at the thought of how easily they all could have perished in a tragic Christmas Eve house fire.

Under the tree were presents for Dad and his brothers: Big Chief paper tablets, pencils, new overalls, and more oranges. While they savored their haul, their less fortunate Grabau cousins dived into their own gifts: second-hand clothing from the church poor-box, canned goods, and oranges. (I find the abundance of, and enthusiasm for, citrus among Lutherans at Christmas slightly peculiar. Some people still insist that children have oranges in their church goodie bags.)

Every year, the men took turns playing der Weihnachtsmann— Santa Claus. If there was one thing my dad, his brothers, and their cousins believed in as much as Jesus, it was Santa. On Christmas Eve, my grandpa or an uncle trotted out the moth-eaten costume that, once donned, hung from his wiry farmer's body. The kids' imaginations had to have been working overtime to believe this was Santa.

Santa 1937, Uncle Al, provided the kids with a particularly unforgettable Christmas. He entered the parlor booming greetings, his hybrid German-American-Nebraskan accent apparently unrecognizable. Dad's cousin, Wendel, excited and on a hard-candy high, bumped into the fiery tree.

"Wendel was a sturdy kid, and he was elbowing me," my dad recalled. "He didn't mean any harm, but the tree started swaying."

Wendel didn't realize that his dad was Santa, and Santa was ticked. Still in character, Uncle Al grabbed Wendel and dragged him to the dining room where he spanked, slapped, and berated his son. The other children quickly concluded Santa was one mean #&*!%@ and the "be good or else" admonitions from their parents were not some convenient tales told to keep them in line.

Disappointment wasn't new to Wendel. His family couldn't make a success of farming, and they rarely had enough to eat. My dad told me how Wendel's family often showed up at the Kuhlmann house at dinnertime, crowding around a kitchen table heaped with pork chops, mashed potatoes, vegetables, and bread.

"I'm surprised our cousins didn't hate us," Dad said. "That's the only time I've ever seen someone's mouth literally water."

Unable to feed his kids in Chester, Uncle Al moved the family west, where Wendel's temper proved equal to that of his father. Wendel's aggression had been limited previously to beating up some schoolboys who were picking on my dad, but in Montana it manifested as assault when he went too far in a bar fight and ended up in jail. Dad often spoke of Wendel's poverty and anger. He had a soft spot for the boy who, on the walk home from school, threw down his books and defended his young cousin from bullies.

I used to romanticize Wendel and his adversity. This was partly my mom's fault. Many of her best Christmas gifts to me were age-inappropriate books. When I was thirteen, she gave me a copy of *The Thorn Birds*, the story of a hot, but taboo, love affair between Catholic priest Father Ralph and the much younger Meggie Cleary set against the backdrop of Australian sheep country. Meggie's half-brother, Frank, has anger issues stemming from the dark secret of his paternity, and he is imprisoned for beating a man to death.[1] When I first read the book, I pictured Wendel in Frank's shoes, rotting away in prison while his family engaged in deceit and forbidden desire. In reality, they were probably fixing cars and canning tomatoes, but a girl can dream. I showed my mom the part in the book that describes Frank's incarceration.

"It's just like Dad's cousin Wendel!"

"Don't be ridiculous, Karen Ann," my mom said. "Wendel isn't Catholic!"

The Kuhlmann and Grabau kids couldn't let down their guard after Christmas because they had to watch out for Knecht Ruprecht. Knecht Ruprecht is der Weihnachtsmann's right-hand man. He's an evil German farmhand who isn't afraid to get his hands dirty while Santa doles out treats. Per German folklore, Knecht Ruprecht wanders the countryside asking children if they know how to pray. If they answer in the affirmative, he rewards them with apples, nuts, and gingerbread. If the children do not know how to pray, Knecht Ruprecht gently teaches them about their Savior. Not really. He screams at them and beats their heads with a bag of ashes.[2] According to Kuhlmann family tradition, Knecht Ruprecht lurks in the shadows from Christmas until January 6, the start of Epiphany. If you have been bad, he will take away your toys and replace them with sticks and coal. If your behavior is truly egregious, he will emerge from the shadows and beat you senseless. German Christmas can be remarkably scary and law-oriented.

Whenever my dad talked about his childhood Christmas experiences, he cried from laughter. He was, from a young age, able to recognize the irony of a vengeful Santa mixed into the celebration of Emmanuel—God with us. It also helped my dad that his parents, though strict, were humble, gentle people who spoke softly, worked hard, and refrained from lecturing their children about money—or rather the lack of it.

꒤

Despite her family's hardship, Mom did get Christmas gifts during her childhood, but she would have instead preferred recrimination-free holidays. When she received her first doll, her father coated it with a fine patina of guilt.

"Thank you for the doll, Daddy."

"Do you know how much that doll cost and how long I had to work to pay for it?" her father asked his six-year-old daughter. "It's ridiculous to pay that much for a toy. Well, now that you have it, go play with it."

Another Christmas, Mom and her siblings received a checkers set. It's not surprising that five kids under the age of ten started squabbling over whose turn it was to play. Without hesitation, their father scooped up the game and threw it into the wood-burning stove, scaring my mom, her brother, and her sisters. Christmas isn't supposed to be frightening. Isn't it all about peace, love, and joy?

꒤

When I was a kid, I loved the lure of the Sears and Montgomery Ward Christmas catalogs and waited impatiently for the mail after

All is Calm?

Thanksgiving. When the catalogs arrived, I grabbed them before anyone else had the chance and, with pencil and paper, plunked myself down on the floor to make my Christmas list, which was usually a variation of the following:

- Bonnie Bell Lip Smackers—no green apple

- Knockers (I knew my parents wouldn't buy me this deadly toy, but we did have an equally, if not more, lethal lawn dart set, so it couldn't hurt to ask.)

- New jump rope

- Barbie clothes

- Store-bought clothes for me

- Love's Baby Soft cologne

- Partridge Family lunch box

- Lite Brite

- NO embroidery floss!

It irked my mom when I crawled under the Christmas tree, counted my gifts, and asked why I had only eight presents to my brother's nine.

"Don't be greedy, Karen Ann," she admonished. "Good things come in small packages." I never appreciated that phrase.

"I didn't say anything about the *size* of the packages," I protested. "I only said Brent has more than me!"

"You should live in China," Mom scolded, "then you'd be grateful for *one* present."

I couldn't stand those goody-two-shoes Chinese kids who were grateful for their meager possessions and cleaned their plates at every meal. (Note to self: stop telling son how good he has it compared to 99.9 percent of the world. It's not an effective parenting tool.)

In truth, I never lacked for gifts under our Christmas tree, and church families blessed us every holiday season. The people of St. Mark in Flint, in particular, elevated holiday generosity to an art form. Flint, as I've previously described, relied almost entirely for its fortunes on General Motors and the vagaries of the auto industry, and the economy was either in the stratosphere or the toilet. But even when the energy crisis hit in the 1970s and people were laid off from their jobs, offerings generally kept up with the church budget, and the congregation never failed to shower love on their pastor and his family.

Gifts started rolling in around December 10th. By Christmas Eve, our kitchen counters were stacked with plates of cookies and candy, and Mom used the dining room as a holding area for dozens of bottles of wine, cases of beer, and enormous gift baskets. There were so many Figi's and Harry and David baskets on the floor that we had to clear a path to walk through the room. The cheese, meats, and libations lasted through the summer. The Brandt family's basket was the most elaborate of all. Gentle Mr. Brandt reliably appeared at the parsonage door by December 20th and handed his gift to Mom. The basket outshone others in size and expense, but he gave it with absolute grace and humility. My mom always protested the basket's grandness, saying we didn't deserve such largesse. One year when she said this, Mr. Brandt teared up and replied, "You are so kind to Beth."

Beth was his teenage daughter and the sweetest kid imaginable. She also was intelligent but about twenty pounds overweight, so girls teased her, and boys ignored her. Beth eventually slimmed down, but it made her not one iota more lovely than she always had been. When I was a child, I thought Mr. Brandt was generically nice to my parents, but now that I *have* a child, I realize he was thanking them for loving his little girl.

In addition to the congregational gifts, there was another perk for Flint pastors at Christmas—the funeral home swag. The burial business in town was generally conducted by one of two enterprises, Brown or Reigle. Every year, during the second week of December, black overcoat-clad representatives from each funeral home showed up at the parsonage door. The man from Brown handed over a frozen twenty-pound turkey that Mom saved for New Year's Day dinner. The turkey was nice, but it paled in comparison to Reigle's annual offering. Maybe it was Dad's fondness for citrus, imprinted on him from childhood, or because my mom didn't buy any fresh fruit except for cheap and abundant Michigan apples. Or did we just need a burst of summer at the beginning of a long, gray Flint winter? I don't know, but when the Reigle guy showed up with a huge box containing scores of juicy, softball-sized navel oranges from Florida, Dad and I both were kids.

"I wish they would give us something practical," my mom sighed as my dad and I tore off the lid. "Like a ham."

Dad and I ate our oranges, feeling like we were mainlining July. We smiled at each other, tacitly acknowledging Mom's madness.

Perhaps my brother often had an extra gift from my parents under the tree because, unlike me, he didn't have a benefactor.

Anna Mae Rohmann first showed up at the parsonage door on my seventh birthday, which, as the reader may recall, was a few days after we moved to Michigan. Mrs. Rohmann handed me a beautifully wrapped package with my name on it. She acknowledged that it must be tough for me to celebrate my birthday in a new place, not knowing anyone but immediate family. If it was okay with me, she would like to be my "Michigan Grandma."

Inside the package was a gorgeous doll—the kind that looked like a little girl rather than a baby. Her carrying case doubled as a closet for her fabulous outfits that included a pink nightgown with ribbons, a blue sweater and ski pants set trimmed in white rabbit fur, and a burgundy riding ensemble. I had never owned a toy as nice as this, and I had met few women as kind-hearted as Mrs. Rohmann. One of her actual granddaughters, Debbie, was my age, and every Christmas and birthday I received the same gift as she did. From an adult perspective, I imagine Debbie might have resented the heck out of that, but her mom, Mary Ann, and her three aunts had the same generous spirit as Mrs. Rohmann, so maybe not. I observed that there was never any condescension or expectation attached to their giving—they just gave.

When Mrs. Rohmann died from cancer a few years later, her four adult girls were a textbook lesson in how to show love among siblings. Standing next to the casket at the visitation, I was shocked at how thin Mrs. Rohmann's formerly plump body had grown before her death. Her daughters were talking to my parents, simultaneously laughing and crying as adult children often do when fresh grief and treasured memories intersect. They explained their desire that, as their mother's death approached, no sister should feel short-changed from having a moment or responsibility that was solely hers.

"I was the point of contact for the family, Pastor Kuhlmann, and the doctors," Mary Ann, the eldest, explained.

"Jerry Lynn picked the funeral hymns and Bible readings for the service, Sharon selected the outfit for the viewing and decided on the luncheon details, and, since Kathleen is the baby of the family, we thought she should hold Mama when she died."

That, my friends, is the kind of Christian example that sticks with an impressionable kid.

❧

Every Christian congregation, Lutheran or not, has its "thing"— an event or quality for which it is known. Sometimes that thing isn't positive. For example, "People are cold and unwelcoming there" or "They blast the air conditioning so high it feels like a meat locker in the sanctuary." But many congregations are known for what they do right, and one of the things that St. Mark in Flint did well was Christmas.

To most people not far removed from their German roots, Christmas Eve is the heart of Christmas. Although Christmas Day is the festival day with Holy Communion, the emotional celebration takes place the night before. At St. Mark, the full congregational service began at 11:00 p.m. The children's program was earlier, at 6:30 p.m. Between services, our family returned to the parsonage to open presents and snack on gift basket food.

In the children's program, each grade level from the day school and Sunday school took turns singing a Christmas song and reciting a Bible verse. It was a big deal when one was finally old enough to graduate from "Away in a Manger" to something more mature like "Angels We Have Heard on High." Every grade combined to sing the final carol. The year I was thirteen, the final song was "The Little Drummer Boy." Miss Hart, our music teacher, was a single, thirty-something who usually accompanied us on her ubiquitous avocado-green autoharp. This evening, however, we sang a cappella. We started softly, singing about the poor boy who had no gift for the Christ child, but we increased the volume when he discovered he could play his drum for the newborn King. We finished in hushed tones, singing about how, as the boy finished his tribute, baby Jesus smiled at him. We had nailed it! The congregation was beaming, and Miss Hart was crying.

"Thank you," she rasped. We sat down, convinced Miss Hart was happier than she ever had been because of our performance. It was a beautiful, peaceful end to that year's program.

Free to go, we raced down the aisle to the back of the sanctuary where the ushers passed out boxes of homemade rock candy and Swedish rosette cookies made the day before by Mrs. Krueger and Mrs. Labrenz. Mrs. Krueger was ancient, and Mrs. Labrenz was her mother. The two widows lived in nearby Genesee where they rented a room to Miss Hart who was a surrogate granddaughter to them. Mrs. Labrenz, closing in on her hundredth birthday, was a Volga German born in Russia back when the Romanovs were living large. She was too frail to regularly attend church (yet somehow found the strength to lift those heavy rosette irons), so my parents frequently visited her. This meant I visited her, also. Mrs. Labrenz, with her wizened, apple doll face, sat in a rocking chair near the fireplace, her tiny body cocooned in a long lavender dress that pooled on the floor. Swaddled in a black crocheted shawl, she steadily rocked and spoke German with my dad while the rest of us sweltered. She seemed even more foreign to me than my relatives.

Between the tales of Knecht Ruprecht, angry Uncle Al as Santa, and lullabies sung to Jesus, I used to wonder if the combination of terror and peace at Christmas was uniquely German and Lutheran. Or was it specific to my family? I didn't know any other kids whose grandparents read them German story books at Christmas in which naughty children, after some mild shenanigans, are run through a grist mill and fed to ducks, after which they are neither missed nor mourned by family and neighbors.

I finally understand that the terror and peace surrounding the holiday are not German. They're a human thing. After all, here on earth, we're still on the B side of eternal life, and I've come to believe that terror and peace are a good fit for Christmas. That's how Matthew's Gospel describes the events of Christ's birth. There's the serene tableau of Jesus in the manger—lauded by angels, worshipped by shepherds, and regarded with amazement by His earthly parents and the wise men who have come bearing gifts. Terror advances quickly, though—at least for Mary and Joseph. An angel tells Joseph that King Herod wants their son dead, so Joseph flees with his family to Egypt. When Herod's soldiers get to Bethlehem, they kill every male child under the age of two.

Years later, in Nazareth, as Luke 4:21–29 illustrates, the adult Jesus reads from the book of Isaiah in His home congregation. At first, the attendees think, "Joseph's son is a decent public speaker." Then they realize Jesus is claiming that He is the One to fulfill the prophecy of a Messiah. That didn't go over so well. The people, many of whom likely grew up with Jesus, march Him out of town with the intent to throw Him off a cliff. Fast-forward a couple of years to the Friday after Passover when Jesus is hanging from a cross. If Jesus' road had ended at Calvary, terror would have won. Grace, mercy, and peace wouldn't have stood a chance. Christmas would be toothless, and eternal life would be hopeless. But that's not where the story ended—in fact, Jesus' story has no end.

Chapter Sixteen

All is Bright

Dad preaching, post-retirement, at Bethlehem
Lutheran Church in Raymore, Missouri, c. 2004

If Christmas often wears me out, Easter does the opposite. Easter is everything to me. It's the fulfillment of every one of God's promises and is, in the truest sense of the word, awesome.

Easter is, I'm happy to say, minimally commercial. Yes, there is candy, and most churches have egg hunts. When we lived in Liberty, the Schroeder family always invited us to their farm for Easter dinner and an afternoon candy hunt. Mrs. Schroeder hid unwrapped marshmallow Peeps and those colorful, cream-filled, misshapen eggs that taste like sugar and FDA-banned substances.

My mom enacted the charade of making me save my stash for later so I wouldn't get sick. However, back at the parsonage, she promptly tossed the candy in the trash.

"You are not eating candy that was on the ground, Karen Ann!" Mom declared. "Goats have been walking and doing goodness knows *what* on that grass!"

My Easter-specific memories are fewer than those of Christmases, but the joy and confidence of Christ's resurrection make it my favorite holiday and my favorite day, period. I love the hymns, too. I'm a weird ranker of things, having spent my life making top twenty lists of everything from best cities (London) to preferred Pop-Tart flavors (unfrosted blueberry), and I've been ranking hymns since kindergarten. Easter hymns take up almost all my top fifteen spots.

"You really like Christmas hymns better than Easter hymns?" I often asked my dad. I couldn't believe he favored the former.

"I've told you this dozens of times," my dad responded. "I like Christmas hymns better, but only because I know there is an Easter." That is, Dad loved singing "O Come, All Ye Faithful," but if Jesus hadn't gone on to die on a cross and then walk out of His tomb a couple of days later, that hymn would be merely an ode to a baby that didn't deliver on God's promise of a Savior.

I can never afford to feel left flat by an Easter Sunday service. Yes, I know the power of the service rests in the Gospel and not the musical accoutrements or the quality of the sermon. The miraculous is worked in the Word and in the Sacrament. I get it. But Christians are human beings who crave wonder and connection to the Divine, and even though we know our relationship with Christ rests on what He has done for us, we long to be moved and delighted.

At Easter in 2007, I needed to be moved and delighted. My dad was sick (he would die eleven days later) and refusing to see his doctor. I'd talked with him earlier in the week, and he had sounded fine. However, when he guest-preached on Good Friday at Holy Trinity, he was barely able to walk to the pulpit. I found him after the service and said he needed to see his doctor right away.

"You think you can make me?" My typically easygoing father was oddly belligerent. Good thing he'd had the foresight to give my brother and me medical power of attorney following Mom's death.

"We both know I can if it's necessary."

By Saturday night he was feeling worse, so I longed for some Easter inspiration.

Jim, our son, and I, along with Brent, who was in town for the holiday, decided to attend Bethlehem Lutheran Church down the street from Dad's house. We had worshipped there a few times when my dad filled in for that congregation's pastor. (There is a shortage of ministers in the LCMS, so retired pastors are regularly called on to preach if active pastors are ill or on vacation.) I wasn't encouraged when we walked into a dark sanctuary. There were no white paraments and no flowers on the altar. Usually, when you walk into church on Easter, everybody is happy and talkative, but not that morning. It was uninspiring, and did nothing to calm my worries about Dad.

"This doesn't feel like Easter," I whispered to Jim. "I need it to feel like Easter today."

He gave the never reassuring, wry smile/shoulder shrug combo he uses to show sympathy and indicate he can do nothing for me.

The service started. A woman dressed in period costume from A.D. 33 ran down the aisle shouting, "He's alive!" A few other similarly dressed people followed her, also yelling out the news of the Resurrection. Normally, I don't go in for costume drama in church, but this was cool. Somebody switched on the lights, and the pastor boomed the Easter greeting, "He is Risen!"; the congregation responded with a roar, "He is Risen, indeed!" The organist began playing the triumphant opening hymn while the altar guild filed down the aisle, bringing with them the white altar paraments and dozens of Easter lilies and other flowers. It felt to me like what the first Easter must have been—a grim and uncertain morning for Christ's disciples until Mary Magdalene showed up with the news that changed everything.

I love the LCMS order of service when, during the liturgy for Holy Communion, the pastor consecrates the elements of bread and wine. The Words of Institution are the same words Jesus spoke to his disciples at the Last Supper, recounted in the books of Matthew, Mark, Luke, and here from I Corinthians 11:23–25: ". . . the Lord Jesus on the same night in which He was betrayed took bread; and when He had given thanks, He broke it, and said, 'Take, eat: this is My body, which is broken for you; do this in remembrance of Me.'

"In the same manner He also took the cup after supper, saying, 'This cup is the new covenant in My blood. This do, as often as you drink it, in remembrance of Me.'"

I'm moved by these words every time I hear them, which in the LCMS is generally every first and third Sunday. They affect me even more when, with a typically packed house on Maundy Thursday and Easter, the wine runs low.

When the pastor notices that there are about one hundred people left to commune and wine left for maybe thirty, he signals an altar guild member to bring more. The woman in charge of that service hurries to the sacristy, where she pours wine into an auxiliary chalice before bringing it to the chancel and handing it to the pastor. Then, and this is what guts me, the pastor unobtrusively repeats the Words of Institution to consecrate the freshly supplied wine. You have to be watching to notice what's going on, but the moment is so meaningful for me. It's invested with the power of the Sacrament, the mountaintop experience of a full church, and, absolutely, the memory of my dad saying the words with conviction and authority.

Every liturgy, creed, benediction, and psalm that loops through my brain is to the tune of my dad's voice. I know Christ's words are what matter, the only ones that cause the miraculous. But it's different to receive communion from the person who calmed you when, at age three, you crushed your thumb in the back door; who baptized you, confirmed you, and officiated at your wedding; who gently advised you to wait on God when the doctor said you would miscarry the long-hoped-for baby you were carrying; and who baptized that same baby who God said would live. There are limits to a pastor's love, and there should be. I've had some tremendous pastors, but they weren't able to show me the love of my heavenly Father in the way my earthly father did.

Both my parents died around Easter—my mom three weeks before in 2001 and my dad two weeks after in 2007. Although I had, prior to their deaths, always loved the holiday, it's even more important to me now. The congregation sang the hymn "I Know That my Redeemer Lives" at both my parents' funerals. Typically sung late during communion on Easter, too, it's often during this hymn that the wine runs low. By verse seven, the Words of Institution are again spoken. As always, I remember my dad quietly speaking them. Meanwhile, the congregation is singing:

———◆◆———

"He lives and grants me daily breath;
He lives, and I shall conquer death;
He lives my mansion to prepare;
He lives to bring me safely there."

—Samuel Medly, 1775

———◆◆———

At Christmas, the tranquility of the manger gives way to the terrifying scene of Herod's soldiers killing the boy babies of Bethlehem. But at Easter, it's the reverse. In the darkness, God flips the switch and banishes fear and death.

I worship in an imperfect Church, and I often am plagued by doubts and worry about too many things: my child's future in this increasingly chaotic world; coronavirus; a headache that must be a brain aneurysm; and that noise on the plane during take-off. You name it, and I fret about it. Christmas, when the cross casts its shadow over the manger, is when stuff gets real—that's why, amid the noise of fake fulfillment, I need some quiet so I can hear what I Kings 19:12 calls the "still small voice" of God. His promise of a Savior, signed in the Garden of Eden, sealed in Bethlehem, and delivered on Easter, rescues us from the mess of sin and from the terror of an eternity without Him. God has cracked open the door of Heaven, invited me in, and shown me what my future really holds. Because He is Risen indeed.

Chapter Seventeen

The Game of Love

My grandparents, Walter and
Hulda Kuhlmann, 1929

Weddings were not my dad's favorite thing. He performed more than six hundred of them during his ministry, and he increasingly disliked how many of the participants disrespected the marriage ceremony. For instance, at one wedding in Flint, the bride and groom knelt for prayer, eliciting laughter from the first several rows of guests. The groom had painted "Help" on the sole of his left shoe and "Me" on the right. During vows at another wedding, the photographer climbed over the communion rail to stand right next to Dad, who stopped, turned to the man, and gave him a look that would kill. The guy took the hint and climbed back over the railing. In addition to people treating the sanctuary merely as a backdrop, Dad had to deal with a cultural drift from solemnity. Historically, weddings in the LCMS included no bride and groom kiss, no popular music, and no clapping. But times were changing.

Beginning in the 1970s, many Lutheran brides decided they wanted to dispense with traditional wedding hymns in favor of more popular tunes. Admittedly, popular ballads can sound more palatable to a couple than these words from a hymn that has been sung at many Lutheran weddings:

———◆◆———

"O blessed home where man and wife
together lead a godly life."

—MAGNUS B. LANDSTAD, 1861

———◆◆———

I'm not saying that a song by, say, Backstreet Boys would be appropriate for a church wedding, but it would be more romantic than a hymn that sounds like it was written for an Amish couple. On reflection, having sung this hymn at several weddings, I think even an Amish couple would reject it as too glum.

❧

Neither of my parents was sentimental about weddings—probably because their elopement was as simple as a wedding gets. They didn't even know the witnesses who signed their marriage license. Photos of my parents from that time show two people clearly in love—eyes locked on each other, arms intertwined, and Mom often sitting on Dad's lap. Three months after they married, my mom was pregnant with my brother. When my husband and I were dealing with infertility, I asked Mom why they had a baby so soon and then waited another ten years to have me. When you are desperate for a child, the thought of postponing pregnancy during peak baby-making years seems like madness.

"Oh, honey, it's hard *not* to get pregnant when you're twenty," she told me, a touch of sauce in her voice. I did not appreciate the allusion to the fact that my parents engaged in any kind of sex life. Ick.

As I've previously mentioned, following my dad's decision to defer his seminary studies so he could marry my mom, my parents moved to Centralia, Missouri, where Mom's family then lived. My mom began teaching school in a nearby town, and her coarse Uncle Vernon hooked my dad up with a job in a brick plant. Years later, when we made family visits to Centralia, I was always uncomfortable with the hard drinking and vulgar language of some of my mom's relatives. I wasn't a sheltered child, but my parents never cursed, and they treated each other with respect. Not only wasn't I used to rude behavior, but I had also inherited my mother's propensity to get all judgy up in your face, so I wondered how my parents could spend time with these people who were nothing like the Kuhlmann side of the family. I couldn't fail to notice how my mom's cousins, aunts, and uncles loved my parents, but watching my dad have a beer with Vernon, who used demeaning language for women in particular, puzzled me. Other family members laughed at and with Vernon, but Dad never did. Having acquired some wisdom (not much, to be honest), I now understand what my dad was doing. He talked to Vernon about life, death, and Jesus—never judging, just being kind. My dad is the only person I've ever known who could be all about the Gospel and still enjoy and be enjoyed by those around him. If you can, with composure, tell your wife's half-drunk uncle that you expect him never again to call his wife a bitch, and that uncle from that day forward not only complies but loves you more for it, then you've got game.

My dad, having grown up with quiet and serious parents, had to learn to deal with people like Vernon, but he was no chancel prancer—that's a pastor who minces around during the church service using exaggerated gestures and a pious voice to appear extra devout. My dad's generation of pastors, probably because they grew up in harder times, seemed tougher than many pastors today. A thick skin is necessary to be a pastor, but so is a tender heart. I couldn't believe my dad put up with a man like Vernon, but I realize now I was witnessing love in action. The whole "What Would Jesus Do?" thing—it's hard to live up to that standard. But my dad's example reminds me Jesus didn't walk up to sinners, tell them to change their ways, and grab a sandwich with them once they repented. No, they had dinner first and established a relationship—then Jesus gave them everlasting bread.

Although my dad was patient with Vernon's rough edges, he did not put up with the cheapening of the wedding ceremony. I was too young to remember any weddings I attended in Westgate or Liberty, but I imagine they were sober affairs. Everything about church was more formal then. Women wore hats and gloves to church. Hat boxes lined my mom's closet shelf, and she kept in her top dresser drawer a quilted aqua glove box. I used to sneak away while Mom was canning or dusting and try on several pairs of her gloves, some of which were elbow-length on her but, on me, reached the shoulder. Most women, including me, don't even wear dresses to church anymore. In fact, I catch myself wondering on Sunday mornings if I can get away with my "formal" yoga pants.

By the time we moved to Michigan in 1971, weddings and church attire were evolving toward informality, and that's when my dad started becoming exasperated. The traditional wedding order of service was, in most instances, no longer relevant to the love shared between wannabe flower child brides and grooms. Admittedly, the vows in the LCMS at that time were old-fashioned. Brides and grooms in the 1970s still plighted each other their troths. If one were to walk up to a twenty-five-year-old today and say, "I want to plight you my troth," they might think you are making a threat or a sexual overture.

Plighting one's troth is a promise of truth, loyalty, and fidelity— pretty good stuff. Many brides and grooms in Flint didn't think so, however. They instead wanted to promise things like "forever friendship," "living in love while giving each other space to grow," and "mutual emotional support while we pursue our separate dreams." In truth, promising to "eat cereal or bring home Chinese on the nights you don't feel like cooking" is a more useful, realistic vow than that gobbledygook. When my dad informed any given couple that they would use the standard-issue vows if they wanted to be married in the sanctuary instead of in a field of wildflowers or by a justice of the peace, invariably the couple whined, "We just want the church wedding of our dreams!"

One of Jim's and my favorite weddings had nothing to do with the couple but everything to do with the song choices, which were sung by the worst soloist we had ever heard. The bride's uncle opened the service with a caterwauling version of "Forever and Ever, Amen." We were close enough to the front to hear the best man say to his brother, the groom, "This guy is terrible."

"It's his best song," the groom answered. "Wait until you hear the next one."

The "next one" was the love theme to *Robin Hood: Prince of Thieves,* and everyone in the pews did our best to stifle laughter as we watched the wedding party struggle to maintain composure.

Disagreements with brides- and grooms-to-be over what constituted appropriate music were another reason why my dad wasn't keen on weddings. In the 1970s, brides were increasingly influenced by TV and cinema weddings, both of which favored the sentimental over the sacred. Onscreen bridal processionals were accompanied by Richard Wagner's "Wedding March" from his opera *Lohengrin,* which, being a German work, has a tragic ending. Many brides didn't even want the congregation to sing a hymn during their weddings. They wanted popular music that spoke of real, deep love. Songs like The Stylistics' "You Make Me Feel Brand New." That's what Sarah Goehner wanted to be sung at her wedding. Sarah was in my brother's graduating class at Kearsley High School, and she was the gold standard of kindness among the under-twenty-five crowd at St. Mark. Her parents had an in-ground swimming pool, and on fifty-degree summer mornings, Sarah gave me swimming lessons. My dad had a soft spot for Sarah, but that didn't stop him from ruining her wedding by disallowing her favorite song.

"There's nothing bad in the song," Sarah argued.

"I agree," Dad said. "It's great to listen to in the car but not in church."

Other songs over the years for which brides tried, and failed, to get my dad's stamp of approval included "Something," "Killing Me Softly," "Time in a Bottle," "Endless Love," and the theme from *Ice Castles*.

If ever my dad's resolve to sustain proper decorum caused any awkwardness with the wedding party, all was forgotten once the reception began. Michigan wedding receptions were a revelation to my parents. These were no cake-and-punch affairs where the guests perched uncomfortably on metal folding chairs, trying to eat cake and peanuts while holding that glass punch cup with the handle too small to accommodate the fingers of anyone over the age of eight. No, these were full-blown parties held in reception halls rather than overly fluorescent or gloomily underlit church basements. Kids were welcome at Flint receptions, during which guests enjoyed a full meal and an open bar. The crowd frequently clinked their forks on the sides of their drinking glasses, signaling they wanted to see the bride and groom kiss. My mom was uncomfortable with this practice, stopping me in mid-clink whenever I attempted to join in.

"Why can't I clink my glass?" I whined.

"Because it's uncouth," Mom mouthed.

After the newlyweds cut the cake, it was time to polka. Polka music was essential at Michigan celebrations, and everyone, it seemed, exited their mothers' wombs knowing how to dance. Most bands played good music, usually German beer-drinking songs. Some couples were fortunate enough to have connections to the state's finest, my dad's old fishing buddy, Marv Herzog, and his band.

Regardless of which band played, there was never any self-conscious hanging back from the dance floor once the music started. As soon as people heard the first strains of "Beer Mug Polka," they were flinging each other around the dance floor in an athletic frenzy. If you walked too close to the dancers, invariably someone would grab you and pull you in for a twirl.

The only wedding reception I remember in Flint that didn't have a polka band was Gina Andersen's. Gina was the daughter of Lyle and Edith, who always looked like they'd fit in perfectly at a Berkeley sit-in. Lyle wore a turtleneck under his sport coat, and Edith was one of the few women at church over the age of thirty who didn't color, comb, and set her hair, preferring a natural look. Mrs. Andersen taught my fourth-grade Sunday school class.

Every week she started out teaching the lesson but sidetracked to politics and world affairs. The narrative about Joseph's bondage in Egypt shifted to a discussion about Anwar Sadat. Anything about Jacob evolved into a discourse on Israel and its role in Middle East violence. (Our teacher was acutely pro-Palestinian.) If the lesson featured someone like the apostle Paul, she tended to stick to her flannelgraph presentation. My classmates and I, bored by a story we had heard dozens, if not scores, of times, waited for an opportunity to steer our teacher off course.

"That's really neat that Paul visited Turkey on his missionary journey, Mrs. Andersen," someone would venture. "Has Yasser Arafat ever been to Turkey?"

Gina, the youngest of the Andersen children, agreed to my dad's requirement for a dignified Lutheran wedding, albeit one that looked like Gina had hired Stevie Nicks as the wedding coordinator. Gina and her twelve bridesmaids were dressed like Stevie from the flower crowns in their unkempt Stevie hair to their lacy gowns and bare feet. They were bohemian-lovely as they glided down the aisle to "Trumpet Voluntary" played on a flute.

I thought their reception was dull. My mom didn't allow me to eat much from the buffet because she was convinced that Gina's hippie friends might drug the food. She permitted me to eat meat and raw, sliced vegetables, things not easily laced with LSD.

"Dad isn't getting high on his plate of food," I pointed out.

"They don't prey on adults, Karen Ann," Mom replied. "Only children."

Since there was no polka music, I sat, bored, on a folding chair next to my parents as they chatted with some Marxist friends of Lyle and Edith's. Meanwhile, Gina and her groom had their first dance to the band's cover of Todd Rundgren's "I Saw the Light."

Naomi Langer and Rick Matthis would date for a few years, break up, date again, break up, rinse, repeat. Each of them was a pastor's kid in Flint. The fathers were Reverend Langer, who pompously insisted on being addressed as such, and Pastor "Call me Gene" Matthis, who didn't worry about titles. Rick was madly in love with Naomi, but she was mostly indifferent to him. Reverend and Mrs. Langer were heartsick every time their daughter, an only child, broke things off with Rick, whom they adored, going so far as to bribe her with a car if she would commit to the relationship. They probably hoped Rick's sunny personality would rub off on their daughter who, from what I observed at pastors' family barbecues, could be a bit of a shrew. Finally, worn down by her parents' entreaties, Naomi agreed to marry Rick. The two pastor dads suggested my dad as a pre-marriage counselor, and when it became clear to him that Naomi was the most apathetic bride-to-be he'd ever seen, Dad suggested a long engagement. He advised Naomi's parents to let up on the wedding pressure, but Mrs. Langer maintained her daughter was in love and suffering from normal pre-wedding jitters. Naomi insisted they "get it over with," so they did.

Rick was ecstatic in the receiving line after the ceremony, so ecstatic that he grabbed me, bent me over his arm, and kissed me on the lips. He did the same to my mom. I was surprised but not weirded out. Rick was a genuinely nice guy, and everybody there knew how long he had waited for Naomi to say yes. The kiss could be chalked up to relief, not creepiness.

Everyone but Naomi had a great time at the reception. Even at age ten, I knew this marriage wasn't going to last. The low point was when Rick, holding a mug full of beer, finally persuaded Naomi to kiss him during the clinking of glasses. He accidentally poured half the mug's contents down the front of Naomi's chaste gown, and she pushed him away, embarrassing everyone. Reverend Langer gave an impromptu speech about patience, eliciting nervous laughter. When, a year later, Naomi announced their split, no one was surprised. My dad used the news as an opportunity to give me some advice.

"Don't marry anyone to please your mother or me," he said.

"She should please us a *little* bit, Marvin!" Mom insisted.

✻

Throughout my childhood, teen years, and early twenties, Mom never failed to school me about my hypothetical future wedding. There was no way *her* daughter was going to have an inappropriate ceremony with secular songs.

"Karen Ann," she lectured when Jim and I were dating, "don't even *think* about having the theme from *Love Story* at your wedding."

"Why would I pick that song?" I asked. "That movie came out in 1973."

"Ali McGraw said, 'Love means never having to say you're sorry,'" Mom said. "That's not true, so you can't have that song."

"I don't want that song," I told her. "I never suggested having that song!"

When you're a pastor's kid, who gets an invitation to the cele-brations in your life? Do your parents invite eight hundred people to your confirmation party? What about a high school graduation party? And who gets a wedding invitation? Everyone at church might not know the pastor's adult child, but everyone certainly knows the pastor. When making out a guest list, where do you draw the line? Many members at Holy Trinity wanted to come to my wedding and reception, but I knew some would rather stay home on a Saturday evening. Mom agonized over the guest list and gave me no say in who was invited. Jim was unhappy because he was given only 150 invitations for his friends and family. When he complained, I informed him that I was given a measly fifteen invitations for my friends and suggested what he could do with his allotment.

Because our wedding was stressful for Mom and, therefore, stressful for me, I felt relief rather than elation when my dad pronounced Jim and me husband and wife. I remember thinking, "Thank God that's over." Jim and I have since regretted that we didn't show up at Holy Trinity one morning, marriage license in hand, and have my dad do a quickie ceremony.

Almost two years after our wedding, Jim and I acted as witnesses at an elopement of two friends. They asked my dad if they could, as we wished we had done, stop by Holy Trinity on a Saturday and get married. My dad, who loved a good elopement, happily complied. We started out in Dad's office where he was watching the AFC wildcard playoff game between the Kansas City Chiefs and the Pittsburgh Steelers. It was near the end of the second quar-ter, and he said we would adjourn to the sanctuary at halftime. I whispered to him that this probably wasn't the scenario Curt and Paula had in mind. Paula overheard and said watching the game was calming her nerves.

They were married at halftime, and we all went back to Dad's office to watch the remainder of the game, after which Dad drove home while the rest of us went out for champagne. It was the happiest wedding I have ever attended, and the Chiefs won 27–24 in overtime.

Chapter Eighteen

Fully Known

My son sitting on my mother's grave marker, 2003

lthough weddings often frustrated my dad, funerals did not. I think when Dad preached a funeral sermon, he experienced a synergy of faith and vocational purpose. People generally don't try to get cute with the funeral service, so there's that, too. Dad really enjoyed preaching funeral sermons even if he sometimes didn't enjoy the reason for the occasion. I say "sometimes" because not all funerals are sad affairs. The death in his sleep of a believing octogenarian is generally not marked by great sorrow in Lutheran circles. In fact, if you were to use the words "tragic" or "awful" at such a funeral, you would be regarded with incredulity and identified as an outsider—perhaps one of those emotional Baptists who weeps far too easily.

The first casket I remember looking into was my Grandpa Kuhlmann's. I was four years old, and my dad lifted me up to see inside. Without drama, or that tense tone some parents use to tell their kids not to be scared but ends up frightening them even more, Dad explained why the body looked so weird. He didn't lie and say Grandpa was asleep. Dad told me the truth. Meanwhile, my mom, terrified of visitations and funerals, hung back. As children, she and her siblings were not allowed to attend funerals—not even their grandfather's. Their parents told them they didn't belong at a funeral because what they would see was so awful it would upset them. Of course, the kids imagined things far worse than reality. Attending funerals was a difficult facet of my mom's role as a pastor's wife. She dreaded any encounter with an open casket and used my brother and me as human shields whenever possible. I remember entering the viewing room at many funeral homes over the years, the canned organ music making Mom even more nervous. When she spied the grieving family next to the coffin, Mom nudged me forward.

"Why do I have to go first?"

"Go on," Mom said, poking my back. "I'll follow you."

She made sure I was firmly planted between her and the casket when she extended her condolences to the bereaved. After a funeral, when people talked at the luncheon about how great the departed looked—"So natural," "She never looked prettier"—my mom had no frame of reference, so, afterward, she asked me for details of the deceased's appearance.

"What color was her dress?"

"Why do you want to know *that?*" This funeral postmortem, as it were, never failed to irritate me.

"Well, she always looked so nice in her light blue dress."

My dad preached a good funeral sermon. This had a lot to do with his public speaking skills but was more the result of his people skills. Dad made it a point to know people. Too many pastors seem to familiarize themselves only with the eternal aspect of their respective flocks. They know their congregants are sinners in need of forgiveness and that sin causes everyone pain in this life. Consequently, pastors too often start with the spiritual, and if that leads them to find out, for example, that this woman keeps bees and gardens organically and that guy plays bass in an Aerosmith cover band, well, that's great. My dad, on the other hand, always started out with the personal. He said he couldn't effectively fish for men if he didn't know whether somebody did or did not like fishing for walleye.

"How can Mrs. Snodgrass (the name Dad used for hypotheticals) trust me to care for her when she's diagnosed with terminal cancer if I know nothing about her?" he said. "My opinion of how she performs her altar guild duties isn't as important as knowing she likes to attend Royals games with her sons and that she wanted to go to nursing school when she was eighteen, but there was never money enough to match her ambitions."

Knowing a person when you are called upon to preach their funeral sermon is essential; otherwise, words of comfort, even those from the Bible, fall flat. The people in the pews want to hear about their loved one, whether that person was their mother or father, their spouse, a friend, or, horribly, their child. The apostle Paul, writing in I Corinthians 13:12 about eternity in Heaven, says, "Now I know in part, but then I shall know just as I also am known." God knows us completely—sins, shortcomings, disappointments, aspirations, hobbies. Why wouldn't a pastor preach about how familiar God is with His child?

When my dad retired from Holy Trinity, the congregation presented him and my mom with a sizeable check to be used for their long-desired trip to Europe. My parents didn't want to go with a tour group, so they asked Jim and me to go with them—as much for the driving as for our company. One Sunday in Salzburg, Austria, we attended an English-language church service that catered to American ex-pats working in Salzburg and a few local Lutherans who desired to improve their English. Worship was held in a classroom building adjacent to the church because the congregation disapproved of the English service, and they judged the printed liturgy, in lieu of hymnals, akin to apostasy. It was oddly comforting to know that Lutherans the world over can nitpick the most idiotic stuff.

Folding chairs were arranged in three rows to accommodate the worshippers, about twenty in all. The large teacher's desk served as an altar. Everyone was warm and welcoming: the young woman married to an Austrian, and her widowed mother who had moved to be near her only child; the young man who, along with his wife and two children, was leaving the next day to begin ministerial studies at Concordia Seminary in St. Louis; and Wolfgang, a twenty-three-year-old theology student who delivered the sermon. His message was about "kennen" and "wissen," two German words that both translate as "to know." They mean two different things, however. "Wissen" means to know something as fact, and "kennen" means to know someone or something intimately. Wolfgang talked about how Christ's knowledge of His children is of the "kennen" variety, and in response to that we, as His followers, need to determine whether our knowledge of our Savior is "wissen" or "kennen." My dad approached Wolfgang after the service, telling the young man that his sermon was "beautifully illustrated," Dad's words for "you knocked it out of the park, kid."

A couple of years later, when Dad attended his cousin Eddie's funeral back home in Chester, he felt the urge for the first time in his ministry to rush the pulpit, shove the pastor out of the way, and give the sermon himself. The pastor was preaching a formulaic sermon that was devoid of "kennen."

Cousin Eddie Stelljes was a slight, bespectacled man, nicknamed "Steel Chest" by my strapping dad and uncles. I finally understood the play on Eddie's name and stature when I was in my twenties. Eddie was a first cousin to my grandmother, ten years her junior and born in Germany, immigrating with his parents to the United States when he was a toddler. He was, like my Grandma Kuhlmann, gentle and soft-spoken. My dad and his brothers loved their older cousin. Eddie regularly drove them to town for a pop or an ice cream, and he turned a blind eye when the boys took his car for joy rides in the fields or on the roads around Chester. My dad was eight years old the first time he borrowed Eddie's car, and he was ten when Eddie gave him his first cigarette. Eddie married another Kuhlmann cousin, Lily Lydia Louise Flathmann, when he was forty-five, making them both doubly related to the family and to each other.

I often was bored out of my mind in Nebraska when we paid visits to distant relations I barely knew—people who didn't own televisions and who kept their curtains drawn and lights off to cool their houses and save on electricity. Two hours in a dark parlor on a 105-degree day following a high-carb Sunday meal at my grandma's house was excruciating, but sitting there hearing the conversation allowed me to acquire a smidgen of "kennen" about those people. They were thrifty, hardworking, and faithful, and their idea of entertainment was listening to swap shows and farm reports on the radio. If a bored child can glean some insight into the character of such people, then an educated, adult pastor should be able to make a stab at it.

At Eddie's funeral, the pastor didn't talk about Eddie as a person. He didn't even talk about Eddie's Christian faith. Not only was there no "kennen"—there wasn't any "wissen" either.

"What did the pastor say that bugged you so much?" I asked my dad.

"It was tragic," Dad answered. "This pastor stood up there for a few minutes and strung together a bunch of spiritual-sounding words that added up to nothing. And it was clear that he never tried to know Eddie."

I heard my dad preach scores of funeral sermons, but two stand out. The first was at his brother Dale's funeral (and wasn't really a sermon), and the second was at his own.

Five months after Dad retired from parish ministry, Dale was murdered—shot as he was heading home for the day from his law practice. As I sat at my uncle's funeral, I thought about how the occasion was a perfect union of my father's ministry through weddings and burials. I recalled my wedding when, during the sermon, Dad observed that Jim and I were "Couple 523" and that "Couple One" was there that day, too. Couple number one was my Uncle Dale and Aunt Ellie. Theirs was the first wedding my dad performed after his ordination, and now, thirty-four years later, he was attending his kid brother's funeral. After a decent sermon by Dale's pastor, people were invited to come forward to say a few words about Dale. Both my cousins, Katrin and Krista, paid loving tribute to their dad, and several other attendees took turns talking about Dale's generosity and sense of humor. One young woman, raw with grief, stood and said how much she hated the unknown assailant who killed such a great man. She went on for several minutes, talking in a quavering voice about unfairness, injustice, and the hate she was feeling. It was probably a good representation of what many people there that day felt, too, but her words provided cold comfort.

My dad had no intention of speaking that day—he was always good about not pushing in on another pastor's turf. I knew, however, that he couldn't let the young woman's bitterness be the takeaway from Dale's funeral. Dad walked to the front and talked about his brother, his childhood partner in crime. He reminisced about their devilment—some of which earned them whippings with a belt and some their parents never discovered. Dad told about how he and Dale used to bribe their older brother, Harland, to act as a lookout at the door to the farm pantry so they could gorge themselves on food meant for the threshing crew. Once, they over-indulged, leaving nothing for the workers, and their mother, who had spent all morning frying chicken and mashing potatoes, sat at the kitchen table and sobbed. Dad told about hunting, fishing, and smoking cigarettes, and he wrapped it up by remembering the day his parents took his infant brother to church for his baptism and how, that day, Dale became God's child. It was at his baptism that Dale received the gift of the Holy Spirit—a gift that enabled him to endure, hope, and forgive in the face of life's complexities and pain. In a few brief minutes, everyone at his funeral knew Dale and knew his relationship with his Savior.

As more and more of my relatives died, I began to fret about who was going to preach my dad's funeral sermon one day.

"Well, it won't be your father, Karen Ann," my mom told me. "He'll be dead."

Thanks for that heads-up, Mom.

It wasn't that I thought anyone other than my dad was inca-pable of preaching a good funeral sermon. My problem was that I had trouble even thinking of other pastors as, well, pastors. My dad had been my sole pastor until I married Jim when I was twenty-seven. Even after that, I still relied on Dad for guidance—spiritual and otherwise.

A few weeks after my dad died, I ran into Audrey Loffredo at the post office where I was mailing death certificates to various investment firms. She and her daughter, both Holy Trinity members, were buying stamps for wedding invitations.

"We're so sorry about your dad," Audrey told me. "Jill is still really upset."

Audrey went on to tell me that my dad had baptized and confirmed Jill and would have officiated at her upcoming wedding in July.

We took care of our respective business and left. Jill wasn't going to have the exact wedding she wanted. I didn't have the wedding of my dreams, and neither did most of my friends. It's an event that is hyped so much that many brides inevitably are disappointed. I wonder how many people experience funeral let-downs?

When my dad died, I recalled his dissatisfaction with Eddie's funeral, and I didn't want the same disappointment with Dad's service. I knew there would be good hymns and great singing, but I wasn't sure about the sermon. I wished my dad could be the one to convey grace and comfort to me, as he always had done.

But do you know what? God is great. *Really* great. And greatly real. My dad's funeral was everything I had hoped for. No, I don't believe God grants wishes. Rather, He gives His children what we need because He knows us and loves us. My dad gave his own funeral sermon, although that wasn't his plan. Two weeks earlier, he was scheduled to preach on Easter, but he was too ill. After dad died, the pastor whom Dad had arranged years earlier to preach at his funeral asked if I had the sermon Dad had planned to deliver. I gave him the handwritten sheets, thinking nothing of it. The day of the funeral, when Pastor Reimnitz announced from the pulpit that he would preach my dad's Easter sermon, I wanted to cry from joy.

Dad's sermon detailed the disciples' fear and despair at Jesus' death, but then told how everything turned around when He appeared to them following the Resurrection, changing their sorrow to jubilation. The conclusion of the sermon was about how earthly separation feels like a jagged knife in your heart when you take that limousine ride to the cemetery, your loved one's body in the hearse in front of you. How hard it is to see that tent and that hole in the ground, and to finally walk back to the car knowing your mom or your dad or husband or child is staying there, and you are going back to your life without them. But, because Jesus lives, everything is turned around. Grief is temporary, and so is that grave.

My trip to the cemetery that day didn't sting quite as much as it otherwise would have because I heard my dad remind me before I entered the limo that everything was going to be okay. What a wonderful gift—it was exactly what I needed.

Gott kennt mich. God knows me. What else would I expect from my Father?

Chapter Nineteen

How I Met My Mother

My mother, c. 1945

Early in our marriage, Jim and I did something monumentally stupid. We assessed the odds of our respective parents' survivability. Bill, Jim's dad, was the oldest of the group but in good health. My mother-in-law was the same age as my dad but in poor health. My dad was reasonably healthy, and my mom was the youngest and most robust of all. It was conceivable she would outlive us. We predicted Jim's mom would die first, followed by his dad, my dad, then my mom. That shows what a fool's game it is to guess at

God's timing because things happened exactly in reverse. In fact, Jim's mom Millie is, while not exactly kicking, still alive.

My mom took great care of herself. She ate double the recommended daily five servings of vegetables and fruits, shunned dessert, and could have stood to gain fifteen pounds. She didn't run or do cardio. Dusting and vacuuming aerobically, she kept fit with obsessive house cleaning. Passing judgment on her daughter's lax approach to housework might have burned a few extra calories, too. Mom ranked a clean house right up there with faith, hope, and love. When my Aunt Phyllis, Mom's sister, died, the family gathered after the funeral luncheon at her Tennessee home. Mom, who adored her youngest sibling, was heartsick. Sitting at the kitchen table, my mom wept as she held my cousin Cheryl's hand.

"Your mother's house is so tidy," Mom observed.

"She cleaned it herself until two weeks ago," Cheryl told her.

"That's wonderful!" Mom exulted.

Fresh from my aunt's funeral, as I sat listening to talk of sweeping and mopping, I wondered if anybody would truly want their epitaph to be, "Her floors were spotless." I certainly didn't and, as it turned out, neither did my mom.

My mom was always on top of her health, except once, and that proved fatal. In 1997, she was occupied with the illnesses and deaths of several family members. Uncle Dale was murdered; my Grandpa Schneller was diagnosed with prostate cancer which, given his age, his doctors recommended go untreated; and Phyllis found out she had advanced breast cancer. Right around this time, Mom had a colonoscopy during which precancerous cells were discovered and removed. Her doctor advised her to report back in two years for a follow-up screening. I'm sure she thought that when she had time to spare, she'd take care of it, but two years stretched to three.

In June 2000, my parents came to our house for Sunday dinner after attending church with us. Jim and I were ready to fly to Boston the next day, where we would rent a car and then travel through New England, Quebec, and the Maritime Provinces. Mom picked at her food, mentioning she hadn't been feeling well. She had a doctor's appointment later that week and was vague when I asked questions. Because my parents had, three years earlier, never told me about the colonoscopy or the results, I left town with no worries.

On July 2, Jim and I reached Prince Edward Island. By this time, our ninth year of marriage, I had dragged my reluctant husband to scores of bed-and-breakfast inns. He was particularly unenthused if they were located in an historic area like Colonial Williamsburg because our room furnishings usually consisted of a four-poster bed with a lumpy mattress, one straight back chair, and a small flashlight we could use to find our way to the hallway bathroom in the middle of the night. If we were lucky, we could read by the meager light given off by the 60-watt bulbs in our faux chimney lamps. We did our best to avoid the hosts who were keen to talk at length about how they had restored the original floors all by themselves. Our hosts on Prince Edward Island, however, were polite but not overbearing. They encouraged us to help ourselves to wine in the communal refrigerator and to relax on the huge wraparound porch with a view of their vast potato fields.

The next morning, after a breakfast featuring a myriad of potato dishes, Jim and I explored the island. We were charmed by the tidy farms, lighthouses, and seas of vivid purple and pink flowers, and we stopped to walk through a field with waist-high blooms. Back in the car and passing a stretch of lupines prettier than the last, I felt a sudden pain in my right breast. The sensation stopped for a few seconds and began anew. I tolerate pain well, so Jim hit the brakes when I started shrieking.

"What is it?" he demanded. "What's wrong?"

"I don't know!" I had never felt such sharp pain. Sudden onset of cancer? It couldn't be a heart attack. Was it my gall bladder?

Lifting my shirt and gingerly peeling back my bra, I discovered two bees pressed up against my right nipple, which had already swollen to the size of a ping pong ball. Bullseye. We found a convenience store, and Jim fetched me ice for the swelling and ibuprofen for the pain. If only this had been the low point of my day.

We returned to our B&B to relax. I lounged on the bed while Jim got comfortable on the straight back chair. Our hostess knocked on our door and poked her head in to say we had a phone call, and Jim left to answer it. He returned quickly.

"It's your dad."

Diligent pastors work hard, and they spend numerous hours, day and night, away from their families. Downtime is rare, and time off is sacred. My parents cherished the couple of weeks each year they could get away, and they respected their kids' vacations, too. My dad was not calling me to chitchat.

"Hi, Dad," I greeted him, sounding breezy, determined to make this conversation insignificant, yet knowing it wouldn't be.

"Your mother had a colonoscopy today."

"Mm-hmm," I responded as though he had informed me Mom was taking a casserole out of the oven.

"She has cancer."

I had no reply to that. Dad would have to talk me through this.

"You are not to cut your vacation short," Dad ordered. "Mom doesn't want that, and neither do I."

"But, Dad," I sputtered before he cut me off.

"It was one of the first things she said. She wants you to have your vacation."

Some people say that but it's clear they don't mean it. They tell you to get on with life and not give them a second thought, but their instructions are conveyed in a high-pitched voice and half-hearted tone that really means "cancel your plans immediately and be here for me." My parents were not those people, and Dad meant what he said.

"Mom's surgery is in two days," Dad told me. "It's going to be okay."

I trudged back to our room and gave Jim the news, and he asked if I wanted to go home. It was a ten-hour drive to Boston, and we could easily catch a flight to be home in time for Mom's procedure. I didn't want to get in trouble, though, so we decided to stay.

After a restless night due to my uneasy mind, the lumpy mattress, and a scratchy quilt, Jim and I drove to Charlottetown where I called my mom who was already in the hospital.

"Hello?" she answered on the first ring.

"Mommy?" I hadn't used that word in over thirty years. We both started crying.

"I will be *very* angry with you if you come home early from your trip, Karen Ann," she told me.

"That's what Dad said."

"He'll be angry, too."

"Okay."

"What are you doing today?" she asked.

"Worrying about you," I replied.

"Well, that's not how I want you to spend the day."

"Okay."

"How's Jim?"

"Okay." My conversation skills were feeble at this point.

"I need you to promise me that you will stay and enjoy your vacation."

"Okay."

"Everything will be all right," Mom assured me.

"Okay," I answered. "I love you."

She loved me back, and I replaced the phone in its cradle before heading to order her some flowers.

I had forgotten it was July 4th until the kind woman at the florist shop, gesturing at my Old Navy flag shirt, wished Jim and me a happy Independence Day. I gave her belated Canada Day felicitations and told her I needed to send to my sick mother the most elaborate vase of pink roses known to mankind. When the flowers arrived at Mom's hospital room in Kansas City, doctors and nurses passed the word to each other that they should have a look at the spectacular arrangement. Dad told me the next day that Mom relished the chance to talk for a few hours about something other than cancer.

"Of course, she's concerned that you paid a fortune for them," he joked.

The following day, Jim and I ferried to Nova Scotia where we stayed at a rustic inn featuring, again, dim lighting and incommodious furniture. Upon our arrival, I called Dad from a pay phone on the inn's property.

"Are you having fun?" Dad asked.

"I wouldn't call it fun," I replied.

"Why not?"

"Dad, Mom has *cancer*."

"Your mother is in good hands," Dad reminded me. "Besides, you know she's an ox when it comes to surgery."

This was true. I had seen my mom bounce back from several procedures, including a hysterectomy and "mild" brain surgery to improve her bad hearing.

When Jim and I flew home at the end of our trip, we drove directly to my parents' house where Mom met us at the door. I had expected to find her weak and bedridden, but here she was, looking fresher and stronger than Jim and I did after a three-hour flight. We chatted for an hour before she asked me to take a walk with her.

"You look really good," I told her as we walked at a brisk pace.

"I don't know."

"Are you scared?" I asked.

"Not about dying," she replied. "But chemo scares me."

"Well, nobody has said you're going to die," I asserted. "Have they?"

"I've worried all along about breast cancer," she said. "I never thought to worry about this."

I knew from childhood that cancer dominated my mom's thoughts. I often spied her checking her neck for lumps or doing impromptu breast self-exams as she stood in front of the kitchen sink doing dishes. Mom believed she and cancer had a date with destiny and, God help me, she passed that disquieting legacy on to me. I live in fear of cancer. I have an aversion to "cancer movies" like *Death Be Not Proud* and *Terms of Endearment,* and I avoid women's magazines during October, Breast Cancer Awareness Month, because the articles strike me as foreshadowing. If I use my mom's logic as a pattern, I will waste time and energy, like she did, worrying about something I can't control.

Back at the house following our walk, Mom settled into her chair in the family room.

"I'll tell you one thing, Karen Ann," she said. "If I beat this, I won't be a slave to this house ever again."

Mom had, long before I was born, chosen to make her house the object of her time and talent. Consequently, every house she and Dad ever lived in, especially the parsonages, were eat-off-the-toilet-seat clean. That was my mom's measuring stick for being both a good mother and an exemplary pastor's wife. Growing up, my brother and I had few chores because Mom was certain we would damage the vacuum, the washing machine or, God forbid, the furniture. Our responsibilities were limited to setting the table and drying the dishes, except for sharp knives which, even as adults, we weren't permitted to touch. Mom also banned us from putting our feet on the furniture. Sitting up straight to watch *Dynasty* was no fun at all. Also, Mom forbade us to leave books or, worse, clothing, lying around. It's probably a good thing she isn't privy to the gross, smelly, post-basketball socks strewn like confetti at my house.

My one other girlhood task was helping with the twice-monthly ritual of ironing my dad's cassock and surplice. A cassock is a long, button-down, generally black garment worn underneath the long, white, bell-sleeved surplice favored by LCMS pastors of my dad's generation. Dad would not have been caught dead in an alb, a type of robe which gained popularity among a few younger pastors in our denomination in the 1970s. An alb is a narrow, white robe tied at the waist with a rope belt—think St. Francis of Assisi. Lutheran pastors who initially favored the alb were regarded by the cassock and surplice crowd as guitar-playing liberals. Most pastors wear albs now, and it isn't the social statement it was forty years ago.

Every first and third Saturday of the month, Mom prepared our workspace by spreading a clean white bed sheet on the floor. She then dusted the ironing board before placing it on the sheet. We removed our shoes, washed our hands, and bowed our heads in prayer. Just kidding—we didn't pray. But the rest of it is legit and felt to me like some ritual straight out of the book of Leviticus.

For the next ninety minutes, I was required to stand mannequin-still, holding the sleeve tips of both cassock and surplice in turn, as Mom attacked every wrinkle.

"Why does this always take so long?" I whined. "I could get this done in fifteen minutes."

"And it would look like you did it in fifteen minutes, Karen Ann!" Mom scolded.

When I would slip into a daydream and forget to use an easy touch, Mom brought me back to reality.

"Karen Ann, you are *crushing* the sleeves!"

Although I had to stand there like a statue, I didn't suffer in silence.

"Why do I have to help iron?" I argued. "It's Dad's stupid cassock and surplice. I HATE this!"

If my dad wandered into the kitchen, where mom ironed close to the faucet in case of an emergency stain, I loudly repeated that he should be the one standing there forever because IT WAS HIS STUPID CASSOCK AND SURPLICE! He always beat a hasty retreat to his study, fearing Mom might get so fed up with me that she would make him take my place.

Years later, after I left home for college, I wondered how my mom was going to iron those robes without help. I had inherited the job from my brother who didn't like the task either but, as Mom regularly reminded me, soldiered through without complaint.

"Who's helping you iron now?" I asked. "Dad?"

"Don't be silly, Karen Ann," she told me. "I'd never let your father help. His fingers are so big he'd just *crush* the material."

"So, all that time, you could have done it yourself?" I asked, peeved about the wasted Saturday afternoons of my youth.

"Didn't we have fun together?" Mom asked.

I wasn't surprised she enjoyed the process. She took pride in my dad's crisp appearance even if the surplice was wrinkled by late service.

"Marvin," she asked at many Sunday dinners, "do you roll your robes up in a ball and throw them in the sacristy closet after early service?"

I realize now that Mom used ironing to spend time with her children. It was our lunch out, movie, or shopping trip—activities that would have required money our parents didn't have at the time. No, I wouldn't characterize those dates with the ironing board as fun, but I smile whenever I recall them. It was a chore I detested, but now I would love the opportunity to spend an hour and a half with my mom. Older and wiser, I'd hold the moments delicately, careful not to crush them or let them slip away.

Mom's house-proud nature reminded me of biblical sisters Martha and Mary who were, along with their brother, Lazarus, Jesus' friends. Luke 10:38–42 gives the account of Jesus' visit to their home, and it has always resonated with me. While Martha rushes around trying to be a good hostess, Mary sits at Christ's feet listening to Him teach, which angers Martha.

"Jesus, you don't seem to care that I'm doing all the work while Mary gets to slack off," Martha complains to Him. "Tell her to get up and help me!" (I'm obviously paraphrasing here. "Slack off" wasn't in the original Greek.)

Jesus gently responds to her rebuke by reminding Martha that she is unduly anxious about getting the sandwiches and potato chips on the table, whereas Mary has chosen the better thing—learning from the Word personified.

My childhood Sunday school materials made clear in their illustrated lessons who was the good sister: demure Mary, slender and neatly dressed without a hair out of place, her beautiful face beaming at Jesus in adoration. Martha, on the other hand, was depicted standing in a doorway, glaring at her sister and Jesus. She was heavyset, her clothing was unkempt and splattered with food, and she cradled an enormous mixing bowl in the crook of one arm while stirring the contents with what appeared to be a twentieth-century, mass-produced spoon.

I always felt sorry for Martha. Rather than taking to heart the message that Mary acted more wisely than her busy sister, my takeaway was, "Mary is a suck-up, and Martha is a frumpy old hag." I made sure to tell my Sunday school teacher, who had feminist as well as socialist views, that Martha got a raw deal.

Even my dad sympathized with Martha. "Somebody has to cook and set up tables for the potluck."

Although my mom resembled the neat, ladylike image of Mary, I always viewed her as a Martha who cared too much about her clean oven but neglected the more important things in life. Too often, we didn't take the opportunity to do something fun as a family because Mom had to dust or do laundry. And it wasn't as though my dad was a male chauvinist, "that's women's work," kind of guy. He consistently volunteered to lend a hand, but, except for the dishes, Mom turned down his offers of help.

"You'll make a bigger mess than the kids, Marvin!"

Despite my Sunday school affinity for Martha, I didn't want to live with her doppelgänger when I was younger, and I now didn't want my mom to spend precious time cleaning. So, if she were going to use her cancer diagnosis as a catalyst to lighten up on the housekeeping, I was all for it.

%

During her six-week recovery from surgery, Mom prepared for chemotherapy. I took her to buy a wig from a shop that catered exclusively to cancer patients. Agreeing that all the wigs were atrocious, Mom and I settled on the least weird-looking one as we listened to another patron vehemently attribute her own cancer to her microwave. Mom was in good spirits. I had forced the wig purchase, but she was relieved she wouldn't have to wear a turban when she left the house—a look she despised because it screamed "cancer patient!"

Mom soldiered through the following four months of chemo. She had a poor appetite and napped every afternoon, but she didn't lose her hair. She had been advised to abstain from coloring her hair, so she went gray and looked great doing so. Christmas passed and, in January, she had blood tests and a CAT scan to determine the success of the treatments. I was at work when she called with the results.

"Karen Ann," she rejoiced over the phone, "I want you to thank God right away!"

"Good news?" I asked.

"Let me read you the report." She rattled off some numbers that made no sense to me. I just wanted confirmation that she was going to be okay.

"Does this mean the cancer is gone?"

"They say there's no sign of it."

You better believe my entire family thanked God right away. Could there have been any clearer indication of His goodness? Everything was going to be all right. Plans we all had put on hold were revived, and the uncertainty we'd been living with evaporated overnight.

Three weeks later, Mom couldn't eat because she was unable to eliminate anything that went into her stomach. Her doctors, unconcerned based on the recent test results, thought that scar tissue from her initial colon surgery was causing a blockage. They admitted Mom to the hospital, scheduling a procedure to ascertain the problem. Dad, Brent, Jim, and I gathered around her gurney in the pre-op area. Surgery makes everybody tense, whether it's due to cancer or impacted wisdom teeth, so we were on edge, but we all believed whatever was wrong with Mom was fixable. A nurse wheeled Mom into surgery, and the four of us settled into the waiting room for what her doctor told us could be an hours-long procedure.

In less than an hour, Mom's surgeon and an intern found us and suggested we talk privately in the hall. The doctor told us that when he had opened Mom's abdomen, he found what looked like a gallon of paint poured into her—a layer of cancer covering every organ. There was no way to remove it, so he closed her up. We stood there, stunned.

"Okay," my dad finally spoke. "What's next?"

We had the option, the surgeon informed us, of a new and aggressive chemo drug. An oncologist would explain it to us later in the week. In the meantime, he encouraged us to remain hopeful.

The four of us, numb from the bad news, found Mom back in her room sleeping off the anesthesia. I sat next to her bed, holding her hand when the tears came. They ran down my face, a steady stream of sadness. I didn't want to let go of Mom's hand and was grateful when Brent gave me some tissues. When Mom briefly awoke two hours later, my dad gave her the bad news while she was still groggy.

"Donna, they found cancer in your abdomen." Dad had delivered enough bad news throughout his ministry that he knew the direct approach worked best. My mom nodded and went back to sleep. Her nurse told us Mom would be out of it until the next day and suggested we head home to rest.

"Dad, are you sure Mom understands what's going on?" I asked as we caught the elevator. "Pretty sure," he answered.

"She was barely conscious when you told her," I protested. "I don't think she'll remember what you said."

The next morning, Jim and I were the first to arrive at the hospital. I had spent several hours the prior evening cutting out hearts and a scalloped border from construction paper so that I could turn Mom's hospital room bulletin board into a Valentine display for the upcoming holiday. My fun crafts, paired with a positive attitude, would work with the new, radical chemotherapy to cure her! I was stapling a pink "I Love You" heart to the board when Mom woke and asked if they'd fixed her digestive issues during surgery. I knew she wouldn't remember a thing my dad had told her. Now I had to be the bearer of bad news.

"Um," I stalled, wondering how to tell Mom that things were much worse than expected. I walked to her bed and put my hand on her shoulder.

"Because of the type of tumor, they couldn't remove it."

"What type?" Mom asked, giving me the biggest side-eye ever.

"I don't know exactly," I answered, lying and telling the truth at the same time. "There's a chemo drug they can use to treat it, though."

My dad walked in a few minutes later, and I found a moment to chide him that Mom did not, in fact, remember what he had told her in her anesthetic stupor.

"Did you tell her what's going on?" he asked.

"I kind of had to," I said.

My dad was a tough, resourceful man. Too often, popular culture portrays pastors as either fire-breathing fanatics or milquetoast wimps. Dad was smart, shrewd, resilient, and patient, but he was from a generation that grew up believing doctors always know best, and he wasn't asking a lot of questions about Mom's care. Neither was my mom. Two weeks after her surgery, she was still in her same hospital room and visited daily by doctors who weren't saying much. The oncologist had not come to talk about the new chemo option. Like my dad, I am smart; but, unfortunately, I am only moderately shrewd, barely resilient, and completely impatient. I was sick of the waiting game and told Dad as much when we met down the hall in the lounge where we convened secret meetings out of Mom's earshot.

"Dad, this is getting old," I told him. "Nobody is telling us anything or making a move to *do* anything." He didn't disagree.

"What do you think we should do?"

"We need to ask if the doctors have a plan because, right now, we're all in limbo."

The next morning, when the doctor concluded his daily visit, Dad and I followed him into the hall. Mom's eyes narrowed in suspicion as we left the room.

"If you think you can help Donna, get on with it," Dad said. "If not, let her go home."

I learned more during my mom's last weeks in the hospital about marriage, honoring my father and my mother, John 3:16, and Philippians 4:13 than I did from a lifetime of church and Sunday school. Our family got up close and personal with the fact that our Redeemer lives. Grace appeared in small moments, like when I walked into Mom's room to discover Jim rubbing her sore, chapped hands. Amid the uncertainty, we managed some normalcy. I reminded my dad about Valentine's Day, and he showed up on February 14 with a paper grocery bag from which he produced a ceramic vase containing a miniature red rose plant, the $14.99 price sticker prominently displayed. Mom was genuinely thrilled.

"I'm glad you didn't spend a fortune, Marvin," she said. "That would have been *ridiculous*."

A person can get so wrapped up in losing a parent that it's easy to forget that your healthy parent is losing a spouse. I thought my dad should have paid at least fifty bucks for what was, certainly, their last Valentine's Day together. But my parents didn't alter their relationship when faced with dire circumstances. They weren't going to ditch their modest spending habits any more than they were going to abandon their marriage vows or their faith, and that supermarket plant was proof of them having been on the same page for forty-eight years. It was with both sorrow and thankfulness that I eavesdropped on them from the hallway a few evenings later as they acknowledged that their partnership was coming to an end.

"Marvin, I don't think I'm going to make it," Mom said.

"No," my dad answered. "I don't think you will."

"We've had a good life, and I don't need to worry about Brent and Karen."

"It has been a good life," Dad said. "I'll miss you like everything."

Mom's oncologist compelled her to sign a DNR form before he gave the nurses an order to administer the radical chemotherapy. The drug was so virulent that Mom began vomiting and having diarrhea the moment the IV solution hit her veins. My dad and Jim had gone down the hall for coffee, and we heard their voices as they returned to Mom's room. She implored me to keep them out, and I complied by slamming the door in their faces before helping the nurse clean Mom and her bed. A few days later, Mom's doctor said another dose of the chemo would kill her, and he ordered an isolation room because her white blood cell count had plummeted.

Two weeks later, Dad asked the doctors to release Mom from the hospital. She knew she was dying and wanted to go home to do it. The social work staff told us Mom would require around-the-clock care, and we were happy and grateful to offer her this last gift. Jim was in Washington, D.C., for work and wouldn't be back for a few days. I called to tell him about Mom's impending release, but he was too busy to talk at length. When he called that evening at 10:30, the background noise suggested he was out enjoying a drink with colleagues while I was doing difficult things. I should have known better.

"Where are you?" I asked.

"Somewhere over Ohio."

"You're coming home early?"

"Where else would I be?"

Jim and I arrived at Mom's hospital room the next morning to find her taking her clothes out of the closet, packing, and, of all things, trying to put in earrings.

"Karen Ann, I'm going home today!" She was childlike in her anticipation, brushing her hair and putting on lipstick.

I rode with Mom in the ambulance that transported her home. When the crew wheeled her gurney up the sidewalk and into the house, she looked, for the first time in months, truly happy.

A hospice nurse showed up to put in a catheter which, let's face it, is uncomfortable for a patient under the best of circumstances. It was excruciating for Mom. She grimaced as the loud, obnoxious woman attempted to shove the catheter in place. True to the adage about succeeding, the nurse tried and tried again. Mom grabbed my arm and begged me to make her stop.

"Karen Ann, please!"

"It'll be over soon," I said, wishing there was something close at hand I could use to kill the woman who was telling my mother that it "wasn't that bad." I despised Loud Hospice Woman. Even my dad despised her when she failed to show up the next morning with the precious, promised morphine, forcing Mom, who was by now writhing in pain, to go without for several hours. Dad called hospice and demanded a different nurse, and when the replacement arrived, Dad spent his anger on her, saying through gritted teeth that he expected swift delivery of painkillers from then on. The young nurse took it like a pro and proved to be as compassionate and efficient as her predecessor was clueless and irresponsible.

Morphine quelled the pain but caused hallucinations. Mom, certain she saw a rat running around the room and wasps swarming the dresser mirror, was terrified. We tried to convince her otherwise, and she became suspicious of us, as though we had put the rat and wasps in the room to scare her and were now lying about it. We decided to validate her fears. It was amusing to watch Jim pretending to stomp to death an imaginary rodent.

"I got him!" Jim told her.

"Thank goodness," she said, relieved.

Mom had come home on a Thursday, and she knew us until the following Tuesday night when Dad, Brent, Jim, and I sensed that this was the end of her cognizance. It was time to say our good-byes.

Dad prayed, asking for strength as Mom met her death. He told God that we knew He was coming to take Mom to Heaven and asked Him to come quickly. Dad was doing what he did best—reminding us that there was nothing to fear. As he did so, we felt God's presence in that room. I believe we were shoulder to shoulder with angels—the air felt thick with them. I am a Lutheran to the core, and we typically don't say things like that, but there is no denying what was happening. Christ meant it when He said He is with us always, and that night was no exception.

Dad said good-bye first. He kissed Mom on the lips, told her he loved her and left the room. Brent was next, and then it was my turn.

"My baby," Mom said as I grabbed her arm and started crying, unable to be strong like my father and brother. I needed her mothering one last time.

"It's all going to be okay," she told me. That had been our go-to phrase for months. I was tired of saying it, tired of hearing it.

"No, it's not," I objected. "Not without you."

"Yes," she said, with as much firmness as she could muster. "It will."

She told me she loved me and said good-bye.

Mom never regained consciousness, but she lingered for three more days, each of us taking turns sitting with her, wiping her face with a cool cloth, and applying balm to her dry lips. On Friday afternoon, after a visit from my Aunt Barbara and Uncle Larry, the four of us—Dad, Brent, Jim, and I—gathered in the room where Mom lay taking a shallow, ragged breath every minute or so. I sat down on the bed next to her, my hand on her heart, feeling the beats weaken until, five minutes later, they stopped.

I looked at my dad. "That's it."

❦

No one had expected Mom to live as long as she did once she came home. She had bed sores, weighed no more than fifty pounds, and was dehydrated and in immense pain. It was her strong heart, we were told, that accounted for those extra days and hours.

Her strong heart. That was something I didn't recognize in my mom until her last year of life. I suppose I was like most kids, selfish and uninterested in my parents' inner lives. I easily and incorrectly assumed that my mom was forever content ironing my dad's shirts, cleaning the parsonage, or baking something for a potluck dinner. That's what I allowed myself to see. When I wasn't looking, she was fighting her shy nature and mustering the courage to introduce herself and welcome visitors at church. The woman who was terrified of funerals showed up at hundreds of them and found words of comfort for people who were hurting. My mom didn't think very highly of herself, and there were many, many times I also didn't think very highly of her. Shame on me.

The day before Mom's funeral was my thirty-seventh birthday. That morning, Dad handed me a birthday card and present.

"Your mother made me promise last week not to forget your birthday."

During the visitation that evening, I received another gift—insight into how other people viewed my mother. Person after person came through the line and told about how Mom always had time to chat with them and make them feel comfortable.

"She was a real lady," was a common observation.

A lady with a strong heart and a "spine made of steel," as Dad told one of Mom's many doctors. I'm blessed for having known her for the strong woman she was rather than the one-dimensional figure I too long assumed her to be.

Death from cancer is unbearably cruel. As many people know, it's horrific for the patient and no picnic for families who watch the disease wreck, then extinguish, the life of their loved one. Even so, I am a more mature woman and a more faithful Christian because of the courage, strong heart, and faithful witness of my mother during her illness and death. Yes, in her heyday she made a phenomenal Sunday roast and a perfect pie crust. She also never let food splatter her microwave, but she wasn't some Stepford cutout who cooked and cleaned while the important stuff was going on in the other room. When I wasn't paying attention, she was at Jesus' feet learning what was essential.

On the wall in my parents' bedroom, across from the bed in which Mom died, was a plaque given to them by a church member. The words on it were from John 14:2. "In my Father's house are many mansions; if it were not so, I would have told you. I go to prepare a place for you."

Mom is with her Savior—free from illness, sin, and pain. She wasn't Martha or Mary. She was Donna Kuhlmann, forgiven child of the living God. She, too, had chosen the better way. And, at last, she has the perfect home—one she will never have to clean.

Chapter Twenty

Just a Dad on Fridays

Dad on a fishing trip to Canada, 1975

When setting out to write about my life in a pastor's family, I thought it would be a snap to put down on paper who my dad was. I was surprised to discover the words and stories about my mom flowed more easily. Maybe that's because I feel like nobody knew the real Donna, and I wanted to show the complex, authentic woman she was. It's harder to talk about my dad because so many people knew him, and each had their own claim on him and relationship with him. Also, I think, deep down, I wanted to keep a part of my dad for myself—the part of him that was reserved for our family on Fridays, his ostensible day off

when church business didn't intrude as much as it did the other
six days of the week.

Dad began his ministry in an era when it was expected he
put his family second most of the time. He wasn't just my dad at
Lutheran school volleyball or basketball games—he was Pastor
Kuhlmann. My dad wasn't just a dad at my confirmation or wedding—he was the officiant. And when he died, and people filed
past his casket at the visitation, he wasn't just my dad or Brent's
dad—he was their pastor. But perhaps, by explaining who my dad
was, I won't lose that part of him that belonged to me. Rather, I
get to share the aspects of his personality that made him a hero
to my brother and me and a dedicated husband to our mom. And
perhaps what made him special to us is what made him special
as a pastor, too.

It bears repeating that Dad relished life. Each day was, for
him, a delicious bacon, lettuce, and tomato sandwich that you
grab with both hands and don't put down until it's gone and you
have tomato juice dripping down your chin, which you wipe on
the back of your hand before taking a swig of cold beer. Dad's
recipe for a BLT, which he once submitted to the Holy Trinity
Women's League cookbook, called for quality bacon and a slather
of mayonnaise. After Mom died, I pictured Dad eating Kentucky
Fried Chicken takeout every night over the kitchen sink, but he
surprised me by learning to cook, going so far as subscribing to
a cooking magazine. He invited Jim and me over once a week to
taste his creations. Dad's tomato, cheese, and phyllo tart was as
good as anything my mom had ever made. On the other hand,
he didn't have to worry about us asking for seconds of his chuck

roast marinated, then baked, in salsa. I make Dad's BLTs and the tart whenever I'm able to coax some decent tomatoes from my own garden, but it's his recipe for life that I never quite manage to replicate. His formula was distilled to two things: thankfulness and low expectations.

When you don't expect too much, you're not as likely to meet with disappointment. How many women enter marriage thinking that life is just like a diamond advertisement? Raise your hand if you, after watching HGTV for six hours straight, look around your house and find it wanting. Of course, we don't have to stream a lifestyle program for proof that we humans always look for something else, something more. I don't know how immense the Garden of Eden was or how many trees or varieties of fruit Adam and Eve had at their disposal, but however much, it wasn't enough for them.

I remember watching a Chiefs game with my dad, Brent, and my nephew when a car commercial featuring a leggy blonde came on. I don't know if Nathan, who might have been ten years old at the time, was more transfixed by the car or the blonde.

"Remember, the girl doesn't come with the car," Dad advised Nathan.

There are Eeyore-style low expectations, and there are healthy low expectations. My dad had the latter. He understood that no one owed him a thing—no person, no government, and, certainly, not God. (Okay, he *was* adamant that if his tax return said he was due a refund, then the government did, indeed, owe him something.) Life was an overflowing bowl of gravy to my dad and, because of that, he found enjoyment in both the mundane and the marvelous.

Did he love everything and like everybody? No. In Dad's mind, there was no reason for oatmeal, cats, or undefended wide receivers with a clear path to the end zone who touched the ball and dropped it. He detested musicals, too. Watching *Cats* would have been his idea of suffering.

It's a given that Dad loved Jesus Christ above all. His wife, children, grandchildren, and the ministry ranked right up there but were second to his devotion to his Savior. He also adored the Three Stooges, Arnold the pig from *Green Acres*, poetry, Shakespeare, homegrown tomatoes, the book of Philemon, ice cream topped with pickle juice, cold beer, Ford cars, and seed catalogs.

Dad savored the absurdity and humanity of Gary Larson's comic, *The Far Side*. He cut out his favorites and taped them to the wall above his desk at home. I'd catch him doing "the Kuhlmann laugh," head down, one hand pressed to his right cheek, chuckling and saying, "Oh, brother," whenever the comic's setting was in Hell.

And he loved outlaw country music. Johnny Cash, Waylon Jennings, Willie Nelson, Merle Haggard, and Kris Kristofferson. I have Dad's country music CDs copied to the hard drive of my Honda Pilot, and I listen, on blistering summer days especially, to songs that cut to the bone of human frailty and loss: "Folsom Prison Blues," "The Bottle Let Me Down," "Good-Hearted Woman," "Sunday Mornin' Comin' Down," and, because Dad probably felt this every day, "Why Me, Lord?" My dad wasn't drawn to the most successful, the most righteous, or the smartest guy in the room. He had an affinity for the little guy, the screw-up, the loser. He laughed at those "My kid beat up your honor student" car stickers.

Dad was stubborn and didn't like being told what to do. When he had cataract surgery, I drove him to the hospital and waited to drive him home. When the procedure was finished, I was called to sit with him while the nurse reviewed post-op dos and don'ts for his next forty-eight hours.

"I'm going to mow today," Dad told me when she left the room.

"She *just said,* 'no mowing!'"

"She meant with a riding mower."

If my mom is why I care too much what everybody thinks of me, my dad is the reason I think positively about myself. In high school when I was competing in speech contests through the VFW and American Legion, Mom made me nervous by telling me to stand up straight (one of her greatest concerns in life was that I would end up "round-shouldered") and stop fidgeting with my hair, for crying out loud! Dad, on the other hand, told me to get up on stage and give the judges an attitude of "My name is Karen Kuhlmann, what are you going to do about it?"

While Mom was admonishing me to stay away from deep water and commercially made tuna sandwiches ("You will die of food poisoning!"), Dad told me to be adventurous. Go out for the play, try the sport, write the poem, take the trip, introduce yourself, be exactly who God made you, and do it to the full because He came to make this life an abundant one, too. I'm a dreamer because of my dad. Every attempt I've made at something new or scary is because he said I could do it, and every bit of gusto I've grabbed is because of his encouragement. I still won't eat tuna salad in a restaurant, though. My mom wasn't a fool.

Unlike my mom, Dad didn't speak in italics or punctuate his conversations with exclamation points. He wasn't a soft-spoken man, but he rarely raised his voice. In fact, he didn't have to speak to get people's attention. He exuded calm and authority, more so because he didn't seek attention. Dad was a good listener, not rushing to respond so he could hear his own voice. If somebody was better at something than he was, he said so. Dale Sveom, the pastor who followed my dad at Holy Trinity, was, by Dad's ready admission, superior to him at many things, including teaching Bible classes and gardening. If somebody else's talent was going to irk my dad, it was gardening skills, but Dad spared no praise for Pastor Sveom's knack for producing first-rate tomatoes, corn, and jalapeno peppers. My parents acted like Pastor Sveom had split the atom when they discovered he used a Salad Shooter to slice hot peppers for canning.

Where my mom's grace was harder to recognize, Dad's was upfront and easy. I grew up categorizing my mom as Law and my dad as Gospel. This hit home after I took a scissor and cut up the dresser scarf that Mom's Aunt Bertha had hand-tatted for her. If she wanted to keep it pristine, why did she put it on *my* dresser in the first place? I wish Mom would have spanked me because her words broke my five-year-old heart.

"I'm sorry, Mom," I said, crying because she was so angry and disappointed.

"Sorry isn't good enough."

"Sorry is absolutely good enough," Dad explained to her after I told him what Mom had said. "That's the whole point."

I carried the hurt from Mom's temporary unforgiveness with me for a long time, and she probably did, too. My mother was a compassionate woman, but, like so many Christians, she sometimes believed that following all the rules is what keeps everything nice and makes everything clean. I think I'm a hybrid of my parents. Gaw? Lawspel? I try to pray when, for example, I see suffering in the Caribbean following a hurricane or in Texas after a shooting. I attempt to read my Bible so I don't feel guilty when I don't recognize the verses my more scripture-literate friends quote. I'm missing the love-to-serve gene that both my parents possessed, but I say "yes" when asked to bake cookies or chair a fundraiser because that's what I feel I *should* do. Yet, all this striving leads me nowhere, and I can hear my dad's voice telling me to cut it out because It is finished, and *my* efforts didn't get the job done.

Dad, too, injured my feelings, and it was on an occasion I thought would be the apex of my childhood. Many kids today have a birthday party every year, and Jim and I threw parties for our son until he was twelve. For his fourth birthday, we hired a magician. Ten preschoolers watched, transfixed, as Jugglin' Jeff made balloon animals when Jim's dad asked how much we had paid for the guy's services. He was shocked to learn that we had dropped 250 bucks.

"That's absurd," Bill said.

My dad said he thought it was a bargain if it kept a group of children entertained and quiet for an hour.

When I was a kid, I didn't have birthday parties. Mom made my favorite meal, beef stroganoff, and my choice of dessert—Mrs. Harry Reay's Waldorf Red cake, which looks like red velvet but tastes one thousand times better, from the St. Peter, Westgate cookbook. My family sang "Happy Birthday," and, if I hadn't torn into them that morning, I opened my presents. These tame birthday observances were fine, but that's what they felt like to me—observances rather than celebrations. I wanted a party and begged for one the year I turned ten. My parents, who ferociously guarded their privacy and didn't want it invaded by a bunch of giggly pre-teen girls, did not want to host a birthday party. Moreover, Mom feared for her furniture and floors and had visions of girls grinding cake into the upholstery and carpet. But my whining wore them down and they gave in. I could have a party, but it would be in the basement.

Mom provided the refreshments, and Dad was master of the games I had selected—pin the tail on the donkey and musical chairs. It was a lame party, even by 1974 standards. Mom had hung a few purple streamers from the ceiling beams in the chilly concrete basement, and we ate cake and drank Kool-Aid as we perched on the cold aluminum folding chairs Dad had borrowed from church. Despite the austerity, I was having fun until we played musical chairs.

We didn't have a portable record player or cassette player, so Dad used a radio for the game. I've always been competitive, so I was happy that I was in the final two when we were down to one chair. My opponent was my chief nemesis, Darla Nagy, whom my parents didn't want me to invite, but I, for reasons passing understanding, insisted. I was as quick as she and I wanted it more, so I liked my odds of winning. We circled the chair as Dad manned the volume dial, our eyes darting from each other to the empty seat. The music stopped, and we plopped down at the same time, each of us taking up half the chair.

"I win!" Darla yelled.

"No, you didn't," I snapped. "It's a tie. Besides, it's *my* birthday."

"That's why you shouldn't win," Darla spat. "You're already getting a gift from me."

My dad intervened. "Darla, you win this one."

I couldn't believe it! My dad was taking *her* side. She was my enemy, the person who treated me like garbage. If this had been Darla's party and we had both sat at the same time, her mother would have bulldozed me off the chair and raised her daughter's arm in victory. I kept my emotions in check as Darla gloated and showed off the cheap plastic prize my mom had bought. Darla only liked the toy because I didn't win—I was certain she'd be contemptuous of it the minute she left the party.

When all the girls had gone home, I went to my room. I was angry at Dad and disappointed that my party wasn't any more fun than a quiet family celebration would have been. After an hour, tired of sulking alone, I went downstairs where Dad sat drinking coffee at the kitchen table.

"I'm mad at you, Dad," I told him. "Why couldn't I win?"

"I wanted like everything for you to win that game," Dad said. "But she was the guest and it was the right thing to do."

"I don't care about that!" I told him. "I get so sick of doing what's right!"

"I know," Dad said.

"I just feel like I always have to act better than everybody else, and I hate it!"

My dad didn't respond by telling me to get used to life's inherent unfairness, and he didn't say that I had to set an example because I was the pastor's kid. He didn't school me, like Mom would have, about turning the other cheek or the meek inheriting the earth. And he didn't tell me to forgive Darla seventy times seven. He let me vent—about Darla, and about Lutheran school teachers who expected perfect memory work from me, who told me I had to set the example for the class, and who lectured me saying, "Karen, you of all people should know better."

Decades later, I finally do know better. I've learned to ignore the expectations heaped on me and to appreciate my life as my parents' daughter rather than as an archetype. Yes, even though I'm well into adulthood and my dad died over a decade ago, people still tell me, "Your dad wouldn't have wanted you to do that," and, yes, I still get asked to have the prayer. Some of my acquaintances buy me only God-friendly gifts like Christian soap or Christian muffin mixes, and my brother is often given devotionals as gifts when a Lowe's card would be handier. It reminds me of my mom, mystified over where to put the latest piece of religious wall art from a well-intentioned church member.

"How many pictures of praying hands do they think we *need*, Marvin?"

I believe I now have a better grip on expectations—mine and everyone else's. And, also, on thankfulness, the other component of my dad's recipe for a great life. My brother was spot-on when he called our dad a person of prayer. It's a fact that Dad was perpetually mindful of God's faithfulness and blessing. How do I know this? Because a couple of years after he died, I found his prayer journal among papers from his desk. It's a narrow-ruled, spiral notebook in which he also recorded hospital visits and practiced solutions to newspaper word puzzles. Each page-long, handwritten prayer begins with a paragraph of gratitude. For Donna, Brent, Karen, and grandchildren. For health, joy in ministry, people who smile, pennies in the coffee can, gardens tilled before the rain, work, a paycheck, aid in setting the 1991 church budget, a strong back, potatoes and onions planted, roof leak fixed, good sleep, people who show up, fellow pastors, encouraging words from little kids, and, "the list goes on, and I cannot keep up."

Not wanting to invade his privacy completely, I didn't look too far beyond Dad's prayers of thanks to his prayers of petition, but one sticks out: "Give my children reason to praise you." Doesn't that capture the desire of every Christian parent's heart? "Show them who you are, Lord. Make some noise in their lives." It's a great prayer, and I'm stealing it.

I have an old snapshot of my dad taken in 1951. He's dressed in ratty jeans, chest bare underneath a denim jacket, cross on a chain hanging down to his flat abs, and he's taking a drag on a cigarette. He looks tough and cool and, I can't believe I'm saying this, sexy. There's no hint of the stereotypical pastor in him. There would never be a black shirt or clerical collar in his wardrobe. He wasn't comfortable

My dad, 1951

setting himself apart from other people like that. Maybe that's why he embodied Christ's grace so well—not because he was pious but because he was a normal guy. He was James Dean and Jimmy Stewart, the apostles Peter and Paul, and the repentant thief on the cross.

Throughout my messy, wonderful life as a pastor's kid, and pastor's wife's kid, God has given me a reason every day to praise

Him, and my parents gave me a reason every day to follow the Savior they loved and served. Here would be the perfect place to say, "I love you, Mom and Dad, I miss you, and I have so much I want to say to you, wherever you are." But I won't. Because I know exactly where they are and Who they are with. And I'll tell them when I see them again.

Notes

Chapter One

1. Wikipedia, s.v. "Six-Man Football," last modified February 6, 2020, https://en.wikipedia.org/wiki/six-man-football.

Chapter Two

1. Chester High School, *The Bulldog's Tale* (Lincoln, Nebraska: Seright Publication Bureau, 1948), 32.

2. *Luther's Small Catechism* (St. Louis: Concordia Publishing House, 1943), 17.

Chapter Four

1. St. John's College, *The Johnnie* (Topeka, Kansas: Myers Deeptone Yearbooks, 1952), 56–57.

2. Ibid, 58.

Chapter Five

1. "A Snapshot of Life in 1963," CBSnews.com. https://www.cbsnews.com/news/a-snapshot-of-life-in-1963/ (accessed November 20, 2019).
2. St. Peter Lutheran Church, *Favorite Recipes* (Iowa Falls, Iowa: General Publishing and Binding, 1967), 33.
3. Ibid, 143.

Chapter Six

1. Craig, Frances. "The Exacting—and Rewarding—World of the Minister's Wife." *Des Moines Sunday Register,* October 11, 1964, 1W.
2. Ibid.
3. Ibid, 4W.
4. Ibid, 1W, 5W.

Chapter Ten

1. "Flint, Michigan Population History 1920–2017," Biggestuscities.com. https://biggestuscities.com/city/flint-michigan (accessed November 19, 2019).

Chapter Eleven

1. MacPhaden, Jennifer. "How to Make Beer Can Hats With Crochet." eHow.com. https://www.ehow.com/how_7805851_make-beer-can-hats-crochet.html (accessed January 30, 2020).

Chapter Fourteen

1. Merriam-Webster.com Dictionary, s.v. "Hard-Shell Baptist," accessed February 7, 2020, https://www.merriam-webster.com/dictionary/Hard-Shell%20Baptist.
2. *The Lutheran Hymnal* (St. Louis: Concordia Publishing House, 1941), 11.
3. Ibid.

Chapter Fifteen

1. Colleen McCullough, *The Thorn Birds* (New York: Avon Books, 1977), 222–223.
2. Wikipedia, s.v. "Knecht Ruprecht," last modified January 12, 2020, https://en.wikipedia.org/wiki/Knecht_Ruprecht.

Acknowledgments

My dad, Marv, had an infectious love of language, and he encouraged me to live boldly. When I was ten years old, I showed him the draft of a wretched romance novel I had written over a weekend. He gently told me, "I've heard it said that a person should write what they know." Thanks to Dad, I know Lutherans and, above all, I know Jesus.

My mom, Donna, was the strongest person I've ever known. This book would elicit several "Honestly, Karen Ann" comments from her, but I have no doubt that of all the people in my life, she would be the proudest.

Jim, you have supported this project, and me, without reservation. You embody selflessness, integrity, and calm. Thank you for understanding my impulsive nature and my need to dream big. Your snarky asides never fail to make me laugh. I hit the jackpot with you.

BC, you are the sweetest part of my life. There is not a day that goes by that I don't thank God for the miracle that you are. You always have been your own person, and I love that about you. All things. Do yours.

Brent, thank you for filling in blanks and for answering questions where my recollections needed fine-tuning. I admire you for many reasons, not least of which are your steadfast nature, patience, and creative talent. I'm grateful that we shared two tremendous parents and a pretty incredible upbringing.

Laura Mars Hildreth, you are my friend, co-conspirator, and fellow traveler. Memories of the Swiss folk museum, the Katy Trail, and Devon are absolute gold. You have encouraged this project from the beginning. Thank you for giving me a shove just when I needed one. It's Keighley!

Karen Heard, thank you for answering questions and providing statistics, names, and phone numbers. My dad not only esteemed you like a daughter, he depended on you and trusted you absolutely. Both my parents loved you and Mark—and Jim and I do, too.

Elisa Parker, I'm so grateful that we became friends while watching our respective sons play basketball. It's pure joy to share our love of books, period movies, good theater, and The Cure. I admire your grit and determination, and your vote of confidence means the world to me. As do you.

Amanda Pascoe, you are one of the most giving and nurturing people I know. I cherish your friendship and your perspective— and the fact that you, as a former Michigan girl, understand the magical power of Vernors and know what a Koegel's Vienna is.

Elizabeth Denker Wheeler, I knew you would give wise counsel and practical advice. You wrote me a beautiful letter when my mom died, and, to this day, I keep it on my desk. You were walking the same path at the time, and your empathy was a tonic. Thank you, my friend, for your valuable contributions to this book.

Cindy Cox, you are lovely inside and out. Thank you for being a cheerleader for my book. You are fearless in what you believe, and you are deeply kind. When my dad died, you told me, "Love, just love." Same back at you, friend.

Mary B Stoll (no period after the initial, readers), you are my style icon. I wish your kitchen and sitting room were closer, because I could sit there for hours chatting with you. The months in D.C., when I got to have fun with you while Jim worked, were some of the most carefree of my life. Thank you for reading my manuscript and for offering sound advice.

George Stoll, Jim and I always look forward to our long talks with you. From that first dinner years ago to the most recent, we've covered a wealth of topics. Your considerable intellect keeps me on my toes. Neighboring villas in Italy? We're in! As a fellow LCMS PK, I've enjoyed trading war stories. Thank you for reading mine.

Dr. Linda Tucker of Cup and Quill Editing, thank you for your attention to detail and your wonderful sense of humor. Your encouragement has made a real difference in how I view myself as a writer.

Michele DeFilippo, Ronda Rawlins, Brian Smith, and the rest of the team at 1106 Design, thank you for your guidance and expertise in the design and production of this book. You have created some beautiful images, and I appreciate your skill and professionalism.

My HT book club peeps, thank you for reading an early, unpolished chapter of my manuscript. You were encouraging and enthusiastic. I value each of you, and I miss sitting around, eating snacks, yakking, and occasionally discussing the book selection.

J.M. Huxley, you navigated the publishing waters first and provided useful suggestions. I look forward to swapping stories from the writing trenches for many years to come.

My church families have been an important part of my life. I am thankful for the people of St. Peter Lutheran Church in Westgate, Iowa; St. Stephen Lutheran Church in Liberty, Missouri; St. Mark Lutheran Church in Flint, Michigan; and Holy Trinity Lutheran Church in Grandview, Missouri. Special thanks also to the people of St. Matthew Lutheran Church in Lee's Summit, Missouri; and Bethlehem Lutheran Church in Raymore, Missouri.

Knowing my church families so well came at the expense of familiarity with much of my own extended family. Living apart from relatives and not being able to visit often meant that I didn't come to know many of my aunts, uncles, and cousins as well as I wish I did. To my family, each of you has made my life richer and more meaningful. Love and thanks to you all.

About the Author

Karen Kuhlmann Averitt is a writer, speaker, and Lutheran pastor's daughter. Just as significantly, she is the daughter of a pastor's wife. She hopes readers of her book find joy and rest in Jesus—Who has taken our messy lives and made us clean.

Karen loves to read, travel, and binge Netflix. Hiking, bike riding, and gardening are right up there, too. She avoids cooking

Photo: Wendy Cantwell

and cleaning whenever possible. Karen lives with her husband, their son, and two pampered dogs in a suburb of Kansas City, Missouri.

Learn more at www.yellowtabletpress.com.

I hope you enjoyed my story! If you did, would you be willing to take a few moments now and share your opinion on Amazon or any other book review website of your choice? Your recommendation in that format is one of the best ways to encourage other people to read and enjoy the book also. I will be grateful for your reviews, whether you provide them online or to other prospective readers in your own way.

Printed in the USA
CPSIA information can be obtained
at www.ICGtesting.com
LVHW070241260923
759113LV00021B/90/J

9 781734 338027